LOUIS RIEL

JUSTICE MUST BE DONE

Riel, the politician and statesman — From a photo in the Saskatchewan Archives, Regina.

LOUIS RIEL
JUSTICE MUST BE DONE

1979
ASSOCIATION OF MÉTIS AND NON-STATUS INDIANS
OF SASKATCHEWAN

MANITOBA MÉTIS FEDERATION PRESS
300-275 Portage Avenue
Winnipeg, Manitoba
R3B 2B3

Standard Book No. 0-88925-059-6

Publisher
Manitoba Métis Federation Press
300-275 Portage Avenue
Winnipeg, Manitoba
R3B 2B3

Printer
D. W. Friesen & Sons Ltd.
Altona, Manitoba, Canada

PREFACE

This publication was originally commissioned by the Board of Directors of the Association of Métis and Non-Status Indians of Saskatchewan at a Board Meeting in the summer of 1977. The purpose of the study was to bring together all relevant material, both historical and legal, about Riel and his involvement in the Red River Resistance of 1869-70 and the Northwest Uprising in 1885. There is a general consensus in the West that Riel was dealt with unjustly by an incompetent government which made him a scapegoat for its own failings. The Métis people in particular hold this view very strongly and believe that the time has come to right the wrongs of a previous century, by granting Riel a posthumous pardon on the basis outlined in the resolution passed at Batoche on July 25, 1978, page (iv) and following.

After much work was done on this publication, the question of proceeding with a submission to the Federal Cabinet requesting the pardon was discussed in detail at the Annual Assembly of the Association held on July 25, 1978, at Batoche. The resolution outlining in detail the Association's conditions for a pardon was approved by the Assembly. As a result of the approval of this resolution, the Association completed its study and submitted its request for a pardon along with this statement to the Federal Cabinet. As this document is being prepared for publication, the Federal Cabinet has not yet responded to the request. The Association, however, is aware that the request is receiving close and careful study and is looking with confidence to an early decision being made by the Government of Canada.

"Riel and his followers were protesting against the Government's indifference to their problems and its refusal to consult them on matters of their vital interest. Questions of minority rights have deep roots in our history. We must never forget that in the long run, a democracy is judged by the way the majority treats the minority. Louis Riel's battle is not yet won." — Pierre Elliott Trudeau, 1968.

"To say they are a small number of dissidents is not sufficient. We know that the few become the many. If they are men like Gandhi, or in my country, like Louis Riel, they live on." — Pierre Elliot Trudeau, 1969.

Canada
6
Louis Riel

RESOLUTION

WHEREAS Louis Riel was the chosen leader of the Métis people who desired a settlement of their just claims by the Government of Canada and Great Britain before Rupert's Land was joined to Canada, and

WHEREAS the Government of Canada in 1869-70 only negotiated with Riel's government as a matter of expediency, and once having concluded an agreement with the people of the Red River, it proceeded to violate and/or circumvent most of the solemn promises and pledges made to the Métis people, and

WHEREAS one of these pledges was to support the request of the Métis people to the British Crown requesting amnesty for all those involved in leading the Red River resistance, and

WHEREAS the Canadian government, having pledged the personal safety of Riel and his followers, immediately violated this pledge by issuing a warrant for the arrest of Riel for the murder of Thomas Scott, and

WHEREAS the Canadian government by the recognition of Sir John A. Macdonald in parliament had no legal jurisdiction in Rupert's Land, such action by the government was clearly in violation of all accepted legal international conventions of the time, and

WHEREAS Riel eventually had to flee to the United States for his safety, where he resided for almost 15 years and became an American citizen, and

WHEREAS Riel only returned to Canada at the request of his people to lead them through peaceful means to secure for the Métis of the Northwest the guarantee of those rights granted through the Manitoba Act, to the Métis people in that Province, and

WHEREAS Canada had steadfastly refused to either recognize the claims of the Métis outside Manitoba or to negotiate a settlement of these claims, the Métis people, therefore, still had a legal and unsatisfied claim which by the B.N.A. Act and the Rupert's Land Transfer Agreement, the government of Canada had legally pledged to satisfy, and

WHEREAS the Métis people therefore had a right in international law to organize themselves to press for such a settlement of their claims, and

WHEREAS the government of Canada through its continued

refusal to negotiate these claims, and by its police actions to break up the Métis alliance at Batoche and by moving armed troops into the Northwest, forced the Métis to arm and defend themselves, and thus precipitated an armed conflict between the Métis people and the Canadian government known as the Northwest Rebellion, and

WHEREAS Louis Riel, an American citizen, was unjustly detained, tried on a charge of treason against the Crown, was convicted and hanged, and

WHEREAS these actions by the Canadian government were in violation of his rights as an American citizen, and

WHEREAS the trial proceedings were unfair and the public statements by politicians and officials such as Macdonald and Dewdney, that Riel must hang, were political in nature and resulted in a political execution,

THEREFORE, be it resolved that the government of Canada in recognition of these historical facts and of the injustice of its dealings with the Métis people, act to right these wrongs against Riel and the whole Métis nation, by granting at this late date a posthumous pardon to Riel, thereby restoring in the Métis people the knowledge of the justice of their cause and the pride of independence, perseverance, and high standards of their ancestors, and also thereby restoring in the Métis people today their belief in themselves and rekindling their hope that their yet unsatisfied claims will be dealt with justly and fairly and with equity by the government of Canada and the Canadian people.

Passed unanimously at the Annual Assembly of the Association of Métis and Non-Status Indians of Saskatchewan, July 25, 1978, at Batoche.

"In 1885, after the defeat at Batoche, he could have yielded to his people's entreaties and gone to the United States, but he preferred to give himself up and sacrifice his life for the welfare of his people. Riel was a model of self-denial, sacrifice and devotion."

— Tremaudan

"When Louis Riel dropped to his death on the scaffold in the North West Mounted Police barracks at Regina on Nov. 16, 1885, Sir John A. Macdonald and his cabinet imagined they had finally ended the career of Louis Riel and the Métis problems he had fostered for so many years.

But this was not to be. Like John Brown's body, his soul or the ideals he had cherished, go marching on. There was nothing wrong with Louis Riel except that he lived a hundred years too soon."

— George Shepherd, Curator
Western Development Museum.
Star Phoenix, Accent, Nov. 14/78

"Yet in a negative way the cause did live on, for Riel's death and the destruction of the Métis culture represented something in our new world of Canada emerging into nationhood that, a century afterwards, we cannot finally and wholly accept. In this way, while Riel's own will was rooted in the past, his involuntary destiny belonged to the future that in Canada today has become our present, the present in which the disinherited whom Riel still symbolically represents — the Métis, the Indians, the French-Canadians, the Doukhobors, the minorities in general — rise up against the very world that defeated Riel and his past."

— George Woodcock, *Gabriel Dumont*

"He died on the gallows and his nation died with him — his nation, and the dream of a strange empire in the West. The ideas from which the dream evolved live on among the remnants of his people, but they live feebly because the race is weak and dispersed and despised."

— Joseph Howard, an American.

"Whether we realize it or not, we of 1968 face a situation which is similar in some respects. If Riel could walk the soil of Canada today, I am sure his sense of justice would be outraged as it was in 1885."

— Ross Thatcher, 1968

Table of Contents

Statue of Louis Riel by John Nugent, on the grounds of the Provincial Legislative Buildings, Regina — Photo by Cliff Bunnie.

I.

Introduction

For ninety-three years the label of "traitor" has blemished the name and character of Louis "David" Riel. This, however, does not preclude the honour and admiration which has continued to survive in the succeeding generations of Métis and socially-conscious non-Indian peoples of Canada.

Louis Riel met his death on a scaffold in the North West Mounted Police Compound in Regina, Northwest Territories, on November 16, 1885. The crime for which he was hanged was high treason, when in reality and on a human plane, all he was striving for was a just and equitable treatment of the half-breed's rights. This was neglected, as well as the jury's recommendation for mercy.[1]

The springing of the trap-door that led to Riel's death was the beginning of close to a century of doubts, questions and debates as to Riel's guilt, and/or the fairness of the trial. Also questionable is the execution of the death sentence, in light of the loud clamour for mercy by numerous Canadians, as well as the jury's recommendation of mercy.

To the Métis of today, Louis Riel was and has continued to be a national hero and a source of inspiration. His supreme sacrifice has fanned the flames of the national and cultural heritage of our race. A traitor he is not, at least in the eyes of his people. Numerous persons have stepped forward to carry on his struggle for the liberation of the Métis from their past and current subjection to a life of poverty and despair.

Justice must not only be spoken of; it must be exercised. The pardoning of Louis Riel is an appropriate stepping-stone to demonstrate the Government's desire to rectify the long-standing grievances of the Métis.

---

[1]Canada, House of Commons, Debates, 19 March, 1886, at 225.

II.

Purpose of the Submission

As mentioned earlier, there are many questions which have been generated from the execution of Riel. Of course, all of these questions cannot be answered, but several should nevertheless be posed.

Was Riel a traitor or was he a hero? Was he guilty or innocent of the charges brought against him? Was he a sane and rational man acting out of conviction and principle or was he a strange mystic of questionable mental balance as some have suggested? Did he or did he not receive a fair trial? If political leaders and the public of today recognize him as a just man fighting for a just cause, why does the blot of a criminal conviction continue to stain his reputation? Why erect statues to a criminal? Why make a martyr of a criminal? Why revere a criminal in history and in the theatre? Could it be that the majority of Canadians today, as they may have in the past, recognize that Riel was not a criminal and that he was unfairly dealt with? If so, justice demands more than mere recognition of these facts; it demands that the authorities must now wipe clean the slate. This can be done by lifting this criminal stain from Riel's record.

The purpose of this submission is the request that the Government, under the Royal Prerogative of mercy, untarnish the spirit and contributions of Louis Riel towards the rights and freedoms of minorities, by granting a posthumous pardon.[2] We realize that this will be of no comfort to Riel. However, it will be comforting to us, his people, in continuing his struggle, by exhausting all legitimate means at our disposal to secure our rights.

This submission is not a legal treatise to reconstruct the trial and prove Riel innocent. It will instead examine the historical facts and the record dealing with the events leading first to the Red River disturbances and eventually culminating in the Northwest Rebellion

---

[2]See p. 92 for a discussion on Royal prerogative of mercy and posthumous pardons.

and the subsequent trial and execution of Riel. Our primary objective is to show that a grave miscarriage of justice resulted, and that for the future of our people and Canada, this injustice can and must be redressed.

III.

Prosecution and Execution

In order to better understand and analyse events and conditions of Riel's life and stuggles, a brief review of the judicial process which terminated his life, is necessary.

On May 15, 1885, Riel voluntarily surrendered to Canadian government scouts. He was then taken to Major-General Frederick Middleton, who had written him a letter promising protection upon surrender and until the Government had decided his case.[3] General Middleton then provided Riel with an armed guard until he was delivered to the North West Mounted Police Compound in Regina, on May 23, 1885.[4] It is to be noted that Middleton's original intention was to transport Riel to Manitoba, but that he received directives to the contrary.[5]

The Court that conducted Riel's trial assembled on July 20, 1885, and proceeded to arraign the prisoner. The following indictment was read out:

> Sixth day of July, in the year of Our Lord 1885, at the Town of Regina in the Northwest Territories;
>
> Before me, Hugh Richardson, one of the stipendiary magistrates of the Northwest Territories, exercising criminal jurisdiction under the provisions of the Northwest Act, 1880.
>
> Louis Riel, you stand charged on oath before me as follows:
>
> 'The information and complaint of Alexander David Stewart, of the City of Hamilton, in the Province of Ontario, in the Dominion of Canada, chief of police, taken the sixth day of July, in the year of our Lord one thousand eight hundred and eighty-five, before the undersigned, one of Her Majesty's stipendiary magistrates in and for the said Northwest Territories of Canada, who saith:
>
> 1. That Louis Riel being a subject of our Lady the Queen, not regarding the duty of his allegiance, nor having the fear of God in his heart, but being moved and seduced by the instigation of the devil as a false traitor against our said Lady the Queen, and wholly withdrawing the

---

[3]Desmond Morton, *The Queen* v. *Louis Riel,* 1974, at 184-185.
[4]*Ibid.*, at 185.
[5]*Ibid.*, at viii.

allegiance, fidelity and obedience which every true and faithful subject of our said Lady the Queen should and of right ought to bear towards our said Lady the Queen in the year aforesaid, together with on the twenty-sixth day of March divers other false traitors to the said Alexander David Stewart unknown, armed and arrayed in a warlike manner, that is to say with guns, rifles, pistols, bayonets, and other weapons, being then unlawfully, maliciously and traitorously assembled and gathered together against our said Lady the Queen at the locality known as Duck Lake in the said the Northwest Territories of Canada and within this realm, and did then maliciously and traitorously attempt and endeavor by force and arms to subvert and destroy the constitution and government of this realm as by law established, and deprive and depose our said Lady the Queen of and from the style, honor and kingly name of the Imperial Crown of this realm, in contempt of our said Lady the Queen and her laws, to the evil example of all others in the like case offending, contrary to the duty of the allegiance of him, the said Louis Riel, against the form of the statute in such case made and provided and against the peace of our said Lady the Queen, her Crown and dignity.

2. And the said Alexander David Stewart further saith: That the said Louis Riel, being a subject of our Lady the Queen, not regarding the duty of his allegiance, nor having the fear of God in his heart, but being moved and seduced by the instigation of the devil as a false traitor against our said Lady the Queen, and wholly withdrawing the allegiance, fidelity and obedience which every true and faithful subject of our said Lady the Queen should and of right ought to bear towards our said Lady the Queen, on the twenty-fourth day of April in the year aforesaid, together with divers other false traitors to the said Alexander David Stewart unknown, armed and arrayed in a warlike manner, that is to say, with guns, rifles, pistols, bayonets and other weapons, being then unlawfully, maliciously and traitorously assembled and gathered together against our said Lady the Queen, most wickedly, maliciously and traitorously did levy and make war against our said Lady the Queen at the locality known as Fish Creek in the said the Northwest Territories of Canada and within this realm, and did then maliciously and traitorously attempt and endeavor by force and arms to subvert and destroy the constitution and government of this realm as by law established, and deprive and depose our said Lady the Queen of and from the style, honor and kingly name of the Imperial Crown of his realm, in contempt of our said Lady the Queen and her laws, to the evil example of all others in the like case offending, contrary to the duty of the allegiance of him, the said Louis Riel, against the form of the statute in such case made and provided, and against the peace of our said Lady the Queen, her Crown and dignity.

3. And the said Alexander David Stewart further saith: That the said Louis Riel being a subject of Our Lady the Queen, not regarding the duty of his allegiance nor having the fear of God in his heart, but being moved and seduced by the instigation of the devil as a traitor against our said Lady the Queen and wholly withdrawing the allegiance, fidelity and obedience which every true and faithful subject of our Lady the Queen should and of right ought to bear towards our said Lady the Queen, on the ninth, tenth, eleventh and twelfth days of May in the year aforesaid, together with divers other false traitors to the said Alexander David Stewart unknown, armed and arrayed in a warlike manner, that is to say with guns, rifles, pistols, bayonets and other weapons, being then unlawfully, maliciously and traitorously assembled and gathered together against our said Lady the Queen, most wickedly, maliciously

and traitorously did levy and made war against our said Lady the Queen at the locality known as Batoche, in the said the Northwest Territories of Canada and within this realm, and did then maliciously and traitorouly attempt and endeavor by force and arms to subvert and destroy the constitution and government of this realm as by law established, and deprive and depose our said Lady the Queen of and from the style, honor and kingly name of the Imperial Crown of this realm, in contempt of our said Lady the Queen and her laws, to the evil example of all others in like case offending, contrary to the duty of the allegiance of him, the said Louis Riel, against the form of the statute in such case made and provided, and against the peace of our said Lady the Queen, her Crown and dignity.

4. And the said Alexander David Stewart further saith: That the said Louis Riel, then living within the Dominion of Canada and under the protection of our Sovereign Lady the Queen, not regarding the duty of his allegiance nor having the fear of God in his heart, but being moved and seduced by the instigation of the devil as a false traitor against our said Lady the Queen, and wholly withdrawing the allegiance, fidelity and obedience which he should and of right ought to bear towards our said Lady the Queen, on the twenty-sixth day of March in the year aforesaid, together with divers other false traitors to the said Alexander Stewart unknown, armed and arrayed in a warlike manner, that is to say with guns, rifles, pistols, bayonets and other weapons, being then unlawfully, maliciously and traitorously assembled and gathered together against our said Lady the Queen, most wickedly, maliciously and traitorously did levy and make war against our said Lady the Queen at the locality known as Duck Lake, in the said the Northwest Territories of Canada and within this realm, and did then maliciously and traitorously attempt and endeavor by force and arms to subvert and destroy the constitution and government of this realm as by law established, and deprive and depose our said Lady the Queen of and from the style, honor and kingly name of the Imperial Crown of this realm, in contempt of our said Lady the Queen and her laws, to the evil example of all others in like case offending, contrary to the duty of the allegiance of him, the said Louis Riel, against the form of the statute in such case made and provided, and against the peace of our said Lady the Queen, her Crown and dignity.

5. And the said Alexander David Stewart further saith: That the said Louis Riel, then living within the Dominion of Canada and under the protection of our Sovereign Lady the Queen, not regarding the duty of his allegiance, nor having the fear of God in his heart, but being moved and seduced by the instigation of the devil as a false traitor against our said Lady the Queen, and wholly withdrawing the allegiance, fidelity and obedience which he should and of right ought to bear towards our said Lady the Queen, on the twenty-fourth day of April in the year aforesaid, together with divers other false traitors to the said Alexander Stewart unknown, armed and arrayed in a warlike manner, that is to say, with guns, rifles, pistols, bayonets and other weapons, being then unlawfully, maliciously and traitorously assembled and gathered together against our said Lady the Queen, most wickedly, maliciously and traitorously did levy and make war against our said Lady the Queen at the locality known as Fish Creek, in the said the Northwest Territories of Canada and within this realm, and did then maliciously and traitorously attempt and endeavor by force and arms to subvert and destroy the constitution and Government of this realm as by law established, and deprive and depose our said Lady the Queen of and from the style, honor and kingly name of

the Imperial Crown of this realm, in contempt of our said Lady the Queen and her laws, to the evil example of all others in like case offending, contrary to the allegiance of him, the said Louis Riel, against the form of the statute in such case made and provided, and againt the peace of our said Lady the Queen, her Crown and dignity.

6. And the said Alexander David Stewart further saith: That the said Louis Riel, then living within the Dominion of Canada and under the protection of our Sovereign Lady the Queen, not regarding the duty of his allegiance, nor having the fear of God in his heart, but being moved and seduced by the instigation of the devil as a false traitor against our said Lady the Queen, and wholly withdrawing the allegiance, fidelity and obedience which he should and of right ought to bear towards our said Lady the Queen, on the 9th, 10th, 11th, and 12th days of May in the year aforesaid, together with divers other false traitors to the said Alexander David Stewart unknown, armed and arrayed in a warlike manner, that is to say, with guns, rifles, pistols, bayonets and other weapons, being then unlawfully, maliciously and traitorously assembled and gathered together against our said Lady the Queen, most wickedly, maliciously and traitorously did levy and make war against our said Lady the Queen at the locality known as Batoche, in the said the Northwest Territories of Canada and within the realm, and did then maliciously and traitorously attempt and endeavor by force and arms to subvert and destroy the constitution and Government of this realm as by law established, and deprive and despose our said Lady the Queen of and from the style, honour and kingly name of the Imperial Crown of this realm, in contempt of our said Lady the Queen and her laws, to the evil example of all others in like case offending, contrary to the duty of the allegiance of him, the said Louis Riel, against the form of the statute in such case made and provided, and against the peace of our said Lady the Queen, her Crown and dignity.'[6]

The presiding Judge was Lieutenant-Colonel Hugh Richardson, a stipendiary magistrate for and in the Northwest Territories as provided for under the Northwest Territories Act, 1875.

> A stipendiary magistrate was a barrister of at least five years' experience who served as a part-time judge in the Territories, was paid a stipend for the time he so worked, was appointed by the reigning political powers in Ottawa and continued in office at their pleasure. He was, consequently, a servant of the party in power; moreover, Richardson was the legal advisor to the Territorial Governor.[7]

Although no reference is made to Richardson's Orange connection in the current research by our Association, there is a strong statement to this effect made by Auguste Tremaudan in his *History of the Métis Nation in Western Canada.*

> Richardson's Orangeist affiliations as well as those of Justice of the Peace, Henry LeJeune (French in name only), were well-known.[8]

It is also to be noted that the Federal Government endeavored to

---

[6]*Ibid.*, at 3-7.
[7]Howard, *Strange Empire*, 1974, at 507-508.
[8]A. Tremaudan, edited by H. Adams, *The History of the Métis Nation*, at 142.

A drawing depicting the execution of Riel — Source unknown.

retain the ablest prosecutors, headed by Christopher Robinson, Q.C. the son of John Beverly Robinson, "the hanging judge of 1838, who sentenced patriots Samuel Launt and Peter Mathews and others to hang".[9] The assistants on the prosecution team included Mr. E. W. Burbridge, Junior Minister of Justice, Mr. B. B. Osler, son of Reverend H. Bath Osler of York County, Ontario, Mr. T. C. Casgrain, the only French-Canadian on the Government team, and Lieutenant-Colonel David L. Scott, who formerly practised law in the heart of Orangeism before setting up practice in Regina in 1882.

Although Riel was penniless, a Defence Committee was established and this enabled the retaining of able defence counsel.[10] These were Francois-Xavier Lemieux, Charles Fitzpatrick, James N. Greenshields and T. C. Johnstone.

The make-up of the Prosecutors and the Defence was therefore emblematic of and set the stage for one of the greatest political trials ever to be performed in Canada, at the expense of Louis Riel and the Métis Nation.

> In the composition of these two groups of lawyers were elements of race, religion, and politics which were radically opposed. This trial of native by white involved numerous contrasts: East versus West; Upper Canada versus Lower Canada; Ontario versus Quebec; Orangeism versus Catholicism; Anglo-Saxon versus French; Conservative versus Liberal. In other words, the whole nation was represented and intensely interested in this debate. Never before had a situation occurred in which passions, antipathies and even hatreds had been given complete freedom to expose themselves.[11]

In support of this statement is the fact that the information was sworn on July 6, 1885 by Alexander David Stewart, Hamilton Chief of Police. Mr. Stewart had never seen Riel, nor had he ever been in western Canada. He was, however, a member of the Orange Lodge and no doubt was acting on behalf of the Orange Lodge.[12] Surely there is no reason why the information could not have been laid by an individual from the Northwest Territories.

The jury that found Riel guilty was composed of six jurors as opposed to the British tradition of 12. This, however, was held to be

---

[9]Dr. P. Charlebois, *The Life of Louis Riel,* 1975, at 220.
[10]George F. G. Stanley, *Louis Riel,* 1963 at 343.
[11]*Supra,* note 8, at 144.
[12]*Ibid.*

valid by the Manitoba Court of Queen's Bench[13], with an appeal to the Privy Council denied.[14]

There were also other areas of contention such as not enough time for the defence to prepare, hearsay evidence, bias, hostile jury and a complete disregard for the jury's recommendation of mercy. These issues will be discussed in greater detail in the latter portion of the submission.

This, then, represents the events which have become most widely known about Louis Riel. A description of the less known historical background of the life and struggles of Louis Riel will now be undertaken.

THE FIGHT AT SEVEN OAKS, 1816

*From **Seven Oaks** by C. W. Jefferies.*

---

[13]*The Queen* v. *Riel* (1885-93) 1 Terr. Law Reports 20.
[14]*R.* v. *Riel* (1884-85) 10 A.C. 675.

IV.

The Historical Facts

A. EVENTS LEADING TO THE 1869-70 DISTURBANCES

The Métis people trace their ancestry back to the early French explorers and to the Indians of the Plains. According to Tremaudan, their ancestry can be dated 200 years prior to the events at the Red River. They had become an important force in the fur trading empires, of first the Company of New France and later the North West Company. As the Hudson's Bay Company moved further inland they also became an important force in this company's activities. They provided the main labour force for these far-flung trading operations. They were the guides, the interpreters, the traders, the freighters, the procurers of food supplies for the forts (buffalo hunters), the clerks and the general labourers.

By the early 1800's they had achieved a certain degree of prominence in the councils of these companies, and they provided some semblance of law and order under the direction of Métis leaders such as Cuthbert Grant. During this time they participated in and encouraged the competitive fur trade between the North West Company and the Hudson's Bay Company. At this there were a few who had taken up agriculture, some on a full-time basis, others to supplement their natural food supply.

This period also saw an attempt to bring in non-native settlers. The Métis resisted this introduction of Scots settlers by Selkirk, since this was seen as a threat to their traditional lifestyle based on hunting, trapping, fishing and the gathering of wild fruit.

When the two companies amalgamated in 1821, many found themselves in a surplus labour force. They were subsequently encouraged to settle in the Red River area and pursue agriculture. Some settled in areas further to the west on the Qu'Appelle, and the North and South Saskatchewan Rivers and in other suitable locations. The bulk, however, migrated to the Red River where they established a substantial Métis settlement which became the center of commerce, culture and education for this new people, who looked upon themselves as a nation, and along with the Indian tribes, as the possessors of the soil.[15]

By the mid 1840's, they chafed under the monopolistic trade of the Hudson's Bay Company. They were subjected to low prices for their furs, imprisonment if they sold elsewhere; and they had to pay high prices for company goods often of inferior quality. The Métis, with the help of their priests and an educated élite such as Alexander Kennedy Isbister, organized to resist the monopolistic controls imposed by the Hudson's Bay Company. They petitioned directly to the British Crown; A. K. Isbister, who was established as a practising lawyer in England, presented their petitions and argued their case before a hearing established by the British Colonial Office.[16] Although this Committee investigation did not find the charges of abuse of their Charter and of the people by the Company substantiated, they did recommend that the Company's trade monopoly be ended.

Prior to this, in the latter 1840's, the British sent in two military forces to ensure the stability of the Hudson's Bay Company's authority. The first force of 347 men was brought in during 1846 and returned to England in 1848. A second force of 70 pensioners was brought in during 1848 to remain as a more permanent police force.[17]

One of the most influential leaders among the Métis of the Red River at the time was Jean-Louis Riel, father of the more famous Louis Riel. He directly challenged the Hudson's Bay Company's right to try and convict a young Métis for illegally trading in furs. Riel and his followers challenged the court proceedings and as a result the trader was set free.

> The whole question was brought to a head in 1849, when Guillaume Sayer and three others were arrested and imprisoned for trafficking in furs. Although convicted by a jury of his own selection, Sayer was merely dismissed with an admonition, in view of the hostile manifestations of the

---

[15]For a more comprehensive historical review the following sources should be read: George F. G. Stanley, *The Birth of Western Canada*, 1936; A. Tremaudan, *The History of the Métis Nation; Report From the Select Committee on Aborigines (British Settlements) with Minutes of Evidence and Appendix and Index*, Vol. 2, Session 1837.

[16]See Hudson's Bay Company (Red River Settlement). Copies of Memorials and related material; ordered by the House of Commons and printed April 23, 1849.

[17]Charles Napier Bell, The Historical and Scientific Society of Manitoba, *The Old Forts of Winnipeg (1738-1927)*, May 1927, at 33.

A Métis Farm — From publication Tawow.

> Métis, three hundred of whom, led by the fiery "miller of the Seine," Louis Riel père, and armed with rifles and buffalo guns, surrounded the Court House. The Metis hailed the decision as a virtual victory for their cause and greeted the break-up of the court with a "feu de joie" and shouts liberté." The Council of Assiniboia discussed the half-breed demands a few days later, but the control of events had been taken from their hands, and henceforth the fur trade was carried on openly, and in increasing amount by private parties.[18] .

Other changes were manifested at this time. It was decided that future magistrates for the area must speak both French and English. In 1850, eleven new magistrates were appointed, five of whom were Métis or French. By 1857, the Métis had three of their members on the Council of Assiniboia. They had not only achieved commercial freedom, but protected as well their language, culture, freedom of worship and educational system, along with achieving a direct role in the decisions of government and in the administration of these

[18]F. G. Stanley, *The Birth of Western Canada,* 1936, at 47.

decisions.[19] As a consequence, when the charter of the Hudson's Bay Company came up for renewal in 1857 and hearings were held, the Métis did not object, being satisfied with the state of affairs in the Northwest and with the Hudson's Bay Company rule. Canada, however, protested and set forth its case, claiming the complete area under the Hudson's Bay Company Charter.[20]

There was also at this time a threat of American intrusion into the Red River area. During 1856, the Americans established their presence in the area by sending a military force of 200 men to Pembina. This was coupled with a declaration forbidding the Métis from crossing the 49th parallel for the purposes of hunting or trapping.[21] The Hudson's Bay Company, fearing the American force as a possible prelude to an annexation attempt by the United States, persuaded the British Government to send in a third military expedition. In 1857, a company of regulars arrived.[22]

For the next ten years peace continued to exist in the Red River with the Métis being satisfied with the current state of affairs. Prices for furs were good because of competition from American traders. Buffalo meat was in demand by the growing population and the hides were in demand in the United States. The United States also provided some outlets for other products such as fish and agricultural produce. It also provided a source of cattle, seed and machinery to develop the growing agriculture of the area. The agricultural units, however, were based on the concept of the self-sufficient farm (producing for the needs of the family) and not on export. Only the small surpluses were sold or exported and this provided an additional cash flow in the economy.

Although these events were rather favourable to the Métis, they seriously damaged the profitability of the Hudson's Bay Company trade. By the early 1860's, the Company recognized that changes must come in its trade and commerce in the Northwest if bankruptcy was not to result. The British also found that sending military forces to the area was expensive. Further, with the decline of Hudson's Bay Company profits, the revenues realized directly by the British from this trade also diminished. As a result, when Canada and Britain began to

---

[19] *Supra*, note 15.
[20] *Supra*, note 16.
[21] *Supra*, note 17.
[22] *Ibid*.

discuss the establishment of a federated British Commonwealth in North America, they included the transfer of the Northwest and Rupert's Land in these discussions. By the time Britain and Canada had reached an agreement with the Canadian provinces and colonies on the shape of early Canada, the British Government and Canadian authorities had practically reached an agreement on the transfer of Rupert's Land and the Northwest to Canada.[23]

Senior shareholders of the Company had participated in these discussions and had also agreed on the concept of giving up their claim to the area and to the transfer of the area to Canada. *The British North America Act* of 1867 by section 146 provided for transfers of land to Canada.[24]

The only obstacle to overcome now, as far as the Hudson's Bay Company was concerned, was the agreement as to terms of transfer. The shareholders, however, do not appear to have involved the senior employees of the Company in these discussions or decisions.[25] This, of necessity, precluded the participation of the two governing bodies of the territory under Company rule.

The Council of Rupert's Land consisted of four chief factors and three chief traders. The Council, however, was presided over by the Governor of the Company who was appointed by the committee of directors and shareholders. This Council met yearly and made the important decisions affecting trade and commerce in the area.[26] This Council included Peter Dease, Donald Ross and Richard Grant, all of whom had close connections with the Métis community.

Under this Council, operating as a provincial government, was the Council of Assiniboia. The Council of Assiniboia functioned under its own Governor and was responsible for matters of local concern, including inter alia, law and order, justice, religion, education and civil law.[27]

The records show no evidence that either of these bodies were in any way consulted about the question of transfer or in particular about the terms of the transfer of Rupert's Land. In addition, the Métis people, who saw their victory over the Hudson's Bay Company twenty

---

[23]*Rupert's Land Act,* 1868, 31-32 Vic., c.105 (U.K.), s.5.
[24]30-31 Victoria, c.3 (U.K.).
[25]*Supra,* note 18 at 42.
[26]H. C. Knox, *One Hundred Years Ago,* Public Archives of Manitoba.
[27]*Ibid.*

years earlier as recognition of their nationhood and of their right to say in how the country would be run, were never consulted.

Initially the people did not react to the news of the impending transfer. They probably would not have reacted even after the terms of the transfer agreement were negotiated, if the Canadian government had not initiated a number of disturbing and illegal acts in 1869. First, they began work on a road from the lakehead to the Red River, an act which had not been sanctioned and was objected to by the Hudson's Bay Company. Second, they began conducting surveys in the Red River area. Since the survey system was the Torrens system, it cut across existing land-holdings of the people and led to a confrontation between some settlers and the surveyors. Finally, William McDougall was appointed Lieutenant-Governor of Rupert's Land in September 1869, and was dispatched to the Red River to establish his authority.[28]

The appointment of McDougall and his subsequent Proclamation on December 1, 1869, were clearly illegal, as the transfer was not finalized until July of 1870, having been provided for by the Order of Her Majesty in Council admitting Rupert's Land and the Northwest Territories into the Union, on June 23, 1870.[29]

B. THE PEOPLE OF THE RED RIVER REACT

Shortly after Canada made its claim to the territory under Hudson's Bay Company rule, a small number of Canadians from Ontario settled in the Red River area. One of the earlier arrivals was Dr. John Schultz, an Orangeman dedicated to the cause of joining the Northwest to Canada.

> Dr. Schultz was always an active, energetic member of the Orange Lodge. Through his lodge activities he met numerous provincial and federal government officials whom he was able to draw upon for willing assistance. He used these connections to influence even the political decisions of fellow lodge members MacKenzie Bowell and Sir John A. Macdonald.[30]

He and several other Canadians who came with him brought a printing press and started to publish a newspaper, the Nor'Wester.

---

[28]See generally, Dr. P. Charlebois, *The Life of Louis Riel,* 1975 at 30 to 36; Macdonald Papers, Letters of September 29, 1869 and November 23, 1869 to Carroll and Captain Cameron respectively; *Sessional Papers* (No. 25), 32 Victoria 1869, letter from Cartier & McDougall to Sir F. Rogers, January 16, 1869.

[29]R.S.C. 1970, No. 9, at 257.

[30]*Supra,* note 9, at 27.

Riel stops the survey at Red River — Source unknown.

This paper was used to attack the Hudson's Bay Company and the administration of the Council of Assiniboia. They also used the press to advocate the joining with Canada. In short order, they were successful in stirring up dissension between the various elements in the community.

Their activity did not stop there; they also began to defy the established authority in the area. In 1863, a clergyman, Griffith Owen Corbett, was sentenced to six months imprisonment for the attempted criminal abortion of a maidservant. A small group of English settlers organized and stormed the prison, setting Corbett free. The leader of this group, Stewart, was in turn arrested. He, however, was subsequently released by a force of thirty men. The Governor and his Council, fearing more trouble and having insufficient enforcement officers, took no action against this civil disobedience.[31]

Schultz in the interim had become editor of the Nor'Wester and the proprietor of a local store. In the spring of 1867 one of his creditors brought a successful civil action against him. Schultz, however, refused to pay and assaulted the bailiff who tried to enforce the court order. Schultz was then arrested and was to be held for the next court session. Some of his friends assembled that evening, stormed the jail and released him. Although it was agreed by authorities that the judgement against him must stand, no one could be found to execute it. As a result, Schultz remained free to print his paper and to continue sowing dissension in the community.[32]

As the Métis settlers became more concerned about the state of affairs, they turned to the son of the late Jean Louis Riel, to lead them and make their protests known. Louis was well-educated and articulate. However, he had not yet experienced the difficulties and governmental actions which were to convince him that affirmative action had to be utilized. He was, therefore, more trusting of the authorities than was justified. When the surveyors began trespassing on Métis lands in the summer of 1869 and Riel was asked to help, he was not prepared to believe that the Canadians were actually planning to take the lands of the people. He believed that the trespass resulted from a misunderstanding and agreed to go and seek an explanation. He met with Major Boulton who headed the survey party and

---

[31]See generally; Tremaudan, supra, note 8; Charlebois, supra, note 9; Stanley, supra, note 18.

[32]*Ibid.*

explained the situation. He appealed to his sense of fairness and justice. Boulton was sympathetic but said he had his instructions which he must follow.

Sensing an opportunity to stir up more trouble, Schultz organized a meeting on July 29, 1869, to discuss the act by which Rupert's Land was to be transferred to Canada. The organizers of the meeting were advocating armed rebellion. The Métis, sensing a trap, refused to participate in the meeting. The surveyors continued their surveys in the area and on October 11, 1869, began to survey the boundaries of the land of André Nault, a loyal Métis. The Métis assembled and decided to stop the work. They confronted the surveyors and asked them to leave. When the surveyors refused, they were forced to retire by the assembled Métis.

The Deputy Chairman of the Hudson's Bay Company also protested the encroachment by the Canadian government in the form of road building. The protest was registered with the British Colonial Office, which in turn requested an explanation from the Canadian Government. Cartier and McDougall replied on January 16, 1869, justifying from their point of view this government action, as well as challenging the authority of the Hudson's Bay Company in the area, stating, inter alia:

> . . . We, therefore, beg to remind his Lordship that the boundaries of Upper Canada on the North and West, were declared under the authority of the Constitutional Act of 1791, to include "all the territory to the Westward and Southward" of the "boundary line of Hudson's Bay, to the utmost extent of the country commonly called or known by the name of Canada." Whatever doubt may exist as to the "utmost extent" of old, or French Canada, no impartial investigator of the evidence in the case can doubt that it extended to, and included the country between Lake of the Woods and Red River.
>
> The Government of Canada, therefore, does not admit, but, on the contrary, denies and has always denied, the pretensions of the Hudson's Bay Company to any right of soil beyond that of squatters, in the territory through which the road complained of is being constructed.[33]

The Canadian Government did not desist in their road-building construction. Although the Hudson's Bay Company did not accept this challenge to their authority, their main concern was to complete the terms of the transfer agreement being negotiated, on a basis most favourable to themselves. They, therefore, decided to take no action to

[33]Sessional Papers (No. 25), 32 Victoria 1869.

stop the road. The trespass of the surveyors later that year was not challenged by either the Company or the Council of Assiniboia.

C. THE METIS ORGANIZE TO PROTECT THEIR RIGHTS

The events of October 11, 1869, and the inaction of the Council of Assiniboia, plus the lack of any guarantee of the rights of the inhabitants of the Red River by either the Hudson's Bay Company or the Canadian government, led the Métis to act in their own self-interest. Rumors also abounded that William McDougall was to be appointed Governor of the territory by Ottawa and that he would soon arrive to establish his authority.[34]

The first positive step was a meeting on October 16, 1869, at which they formed the "National Committee" with John Bruce as president and Riel as secretary. The Committee met regularly for the next week adopting resolutions to further their ends.

The National Committee also felt compelled to respond to the impending authority of the Lieutenant-Governor as appointed by Canada. On October 21, 1869, the following proclamation was issued:

> Dated at St. Norbert, Red River,
> this 21st day of October, 1869.
>
> Sir,
>
> The National Committee of the Métis of Red River orders William McDougall not to enter the Territory of the North West without special permission of the above-mentioned committee.
>
> By order of the President, John Bruce
> Louis Riel, Secretary.[35]

This action prompted the Council of Assiniboia to meet, and Riel, who was seen as the instigator, was invited to explain the Métis action. On October 25, Riel appeared before the Council in the company of John Bruce. The explanation placed before the Council by Bruce and Riel covered the following unequivocal terms:

1. That his compatriots were satisfied with the existing government and did not want any other;
2. That they did not approve Canada imposing a new government on them without first consulting them;
3. That they had decided not to allow the Governor to enter the country whatever power was behind him, whether the Hudson's Bay Company or the Crown had appointed him, unless delegates were sent to discuss the terms and conditions of his admission;
4. That although the Métis had only a rudimentary education and were

---

[34]*Supra,* note 10, at 60-61.
[35]Sessional Papers (No. 12) 33 Victoria 1870.

The Cairn erected on the Canada-U.S.A. border where McDougall was prevented from entering Canada — From the publication Tawow.

only "half-civilized", they were going to prove soon that they could expel from the country those proclaiming that it belonged to them;

5. That they were well aware of their poverty, and this condition made more odious the treatment being imposed upon them;
6. That no one considered their existence or their wishes;
7. That, when the discretionary power arrived, the English-speaking inhabitants would gather around him and accord him full power to speak and act as master;
8. That they did not want him and that they had decided to do everything possible to prevent him from entering the country;
9. That, in acting this way, they had in sight, not only their own interest, but also those of the whole settlement;
10. That they were sure that they were not infringing on the law, divine or human, and that they were merely defending their own freedom;
11. That they were not anticipating opposition from their English-speaking compatriots and, on the contrary, they were asking them to join and help them preserve their common rights;
12. That they were counting on adversaries among the Canadian element of the country, a condition they naturally expected and were prepared for .[36]

The Council tried to dissuade Riel and the Métis from taking their planned action against McDougall. However, they were unsuccessful and the Métis were joined by Roger Goulet, a confidant of Governor William MacTavish, and William Dease, a member of the Council and A. G. B. Bannatyne, the Sheriff, who was also the brother-in-law of MacTavish. The Métis continued to organize and over the next several months a great number of events took place. Of necessity, it is only feasible to give a bare outline of those events:

— Delegates were chosen to notify McDougall that he was forbidden to enter the country;

— McDougall arrived at Pembina on October 30;

— McDougall set up camp in Fort Pembina and sent Cameron on to Fort Garry. He encountered the Métis at St. Norbert and was escorted back to Pembina. McDougall was warned to leave the country and he did so immediately;

— Governor MacTavish threw his support behind Riel. At the same time, he attempted to maintain a friendly relationship with McDougall;

— Riel seized the *Nor'Wester* and on November 6, printed a notice inviting the English-speaking people to choose twelve representatives to meet with an equal number of French-speaking representatives on November 16;

— The English and French delegates met as planned;

[36] *Supra*, note 8, at 27-29

— MacTavish issued a proclamation which was read at the meeting but it failed to satisfy the delegates;

— The delegates met again on November 17, but failed to reach agreement on a common course of action to protect their rights. The Métis believed this must happen through action; that they must get a guarantee for their rights before the transfer to Canada took place. The English element on the other hand saw this happening by allowing McDougall to take over authority in the country;

— A third meeting of the delegates took place on November 22, 1869;

— On November 23, Riel occupied Fort Garry and at a further meeting of the delegates, the Métis declared their intention to establish a *Provisional Government,* whose objective would be to negotiate with the Canadian government on the rights of the people;

— The English objected to the formation of a new government to replace the Council of Assiniboia. A further meeting was set for December 1. In the interim the Hudson's Bay Company would continue to govern and a Métis committee would be set up to communicate with McDougall and the Canadian government with a view to obtaining an agreement between the settlers of the Red River and Canada;

— Schultz and his followers got busy spreading rumors about Riel's intentions and plans;

— McDougall published a proclamation on December 1, 1869, claiming authority in the area. This proclamation was ignored;

— Delegates met on December 1, and Riel presented the bill of rights. McDougall could enter the territory if he sanctioned the bill. No agreement was reached at this meeting;

— Riel took Schultz and his followers prisoners;

— December 8, Riel issued a proclamation of independence on behalf of the inhabitants. Several days later he circulated the bill of rights and proposed a further meeting of delegates to discuss them;

— McDougall returned to Canada, December 18, 1869;

— December 26, Bruce resigned as president in favour of Riel;

— December 27, Donald Smith, Canadian Commissioner and Hudson's Bay Company officer, arrived from Canada. Riel freed most of the prisoners;

— January 9, Thomas Scott and Charles Mair escaped. Mair returned to Canada. Scott was recaptured several weeks later;

The Provisional Government — From a photo in the Saskatchewan Archives, Regina.

— January 19, a general assembly of the entire population was called. Smith's credentials were presented but they failed to satisfy the people;

— A new delegation of English and French proposed to work out a common agreement;

— Schultz escaped January 23;

— January 29, the first meeting of the forty delegates was held;

— Each parish had elected its delegate;

— Riel again proposed the establishment of a provisional government. The English wanted first to consult with MacTavish;

— A delegation of three met with Governor MacTavish and put two questions to him. Are you still Governor of this country? Will you continue to be?

— MacTavish replied, "For the Love of God, form a government. I no longer have either power or authority." The Hudson's Bay Company had relinquished its charter to Great Britain, November 19, 1869. The Council of Assiniboia had not met since late October. The British had taken no steps to exercise their authority in the area;

— That same day the delegates set up the provisional government of Rupert's Land. Riel was the unanimous choice for president;

— Riel released more prisoners and promised to release others shortly;

— The convention of 24 delegates now set about the task of revising the bill of rights;

— February 9, they met and presented the bill to Smith. He reviewed and commented on it leaving the delegates with the impression that most of the clauses would be acceptable to the Canadian government;

— February 10, rumor spread that Schultz was organizing a party of 150 men at Portage la Prairie to attack Fort Garry and to release the prisoners;

— Riel offered to release the prisoners if the group recognized the Provisional Government. They refused;

— This show of force by Schultz resulted in the English part withdrawing their support from the Provisional Government;

— Riel challenged the English party and they decided to disband their force and send the men home; .

— A party of 48 men returning to Portage la Prairie were arrested by a group of Métis under O'Donoghue;

— Riel decided the Council must make an example of these men. Boulton and three of his lieutenants were tried in the military court and were condemned to death;

— Riel then pardoned the three lieutenants but announced that Boulton was to be executed;

— Just before the planned execution, Riel announced that Boulton's life would be spared if he pledged allegiance to the Provisional Government.

— Boulton agreed, took the required oath and was released;

— Smith agreed to explain the objectives of the Provisional Government to the English party. He did this, allaying their fears, and they once again agreed to participate in the Provisional Government;

— Schultz, now defeated, fled to Ontario;

— The English chose new delegates;

— The Provisional Council met and completed the list of rights and worked on a constitution. They decided to ask for provincial rather than colonial status;

— The delegates to Ottawa were chosen in the persons of Alfred Scott, Father Ritchot and Judge Black. The first two left for Ottawa, March 23, bearing instructions from the Provisional Government. Judge Black followed a day later.[37]

D. THE THOMAS SCOTT AFFAIR

Thomas Scott was one of a number of Canadians in the Red River who were involved in actions of a military nature designed to overthrow first, the government of the Hudon's Bay Company, and later, the Provisional Government.[38] Scott, an Ontario Orange, was not a leader, but a follower in these affairs. He was a stolid construction labourer, known for his anti-catholic, anti-french fanaticism. Twice he was captured by Riel's men, on the first occasion escaped only to go back and join the forces which were being organized against Riel by Dr. Schultz, Charles Mair, Colonel Dennis and others.[39]

---

[37]See generally; Tremaudan, supra, note 8; Charlebois, supra, note 9; Stanley, supra, note 18; Stanley, supra, note 10; Sessional Papers, 1869-1870.

[38]This action by the Canadians has been outlined on pages 21-33, supra.

[39]*Supra*, note 18, at 104-105; *Supra*, note 10, at 112.

Thomas Scott, labourer and sworn enemy of Riel. He was executed by the Provisional Government — From a photo in the Public Archives, Canada.

Scott was recaptured along with Boulton after a decision had been reached by the Canadians to attack and overthrow the Provisional Government. The total number of prisoners taken on February 18, was forty-eight.

> Scott was in prison only a month. He was one of those who escaped with Woodington, Mair and Parker on the night of January 9. He had played a leading role in rousing the people of Portage la Prairie to the desperate venture, described by Sir John A. Macdonald as "foolish" and "criminal", that ended in surrender on February 18.[40]

Riel realized that decisive action had to be taken against the Canadians in order to prevent further occurrences of armed resistance and attack. As Boulton had spearheaded a number of attacks against the Provisional Government, Riel decided to use him as an example. Boulton was subsequently courtmartialed and condemned to be executed. Riel, however, ever vigilant against bloody civil war, pardoned Boulton upon the latter's promise to co-operate with the Provisional Government. Similar grants of amnesty were offered to all other prisoners who promised to be loyal and not take up arms against the Provisional Government again.

The only prisoner adverse to taking the oath was Scott, who felt it was below his dignity to do so.

> Scott merely, "sneered" at Riel and "made fun of" the Métis leader. He had nothing but contempt for all mixed-bloods and to his sense of racial superiority he added the narrow bigotry of the Ulster Orangeman.[41]

Scott was vociferous in his derogatory remarks to his captors as well as jostling and threatening them on every possible occasion. Scott also made it clear that he was a threat to Riel and the Provisional Government.

> Taken a prisoner a second time, it is said that he violently attacked his guards, incited his companions to do likewise and threatened the life of Riel if he ever escaped.[42]

According to the most widely accepted version of the Scott story, he was court martialled and was condemned to be executed. Again, according to the official versions, he was executed, his body spirited away and disposed of by several of Riel's men. They claimed to have buried the body but later, at the request of the family and under military pressure from Wolsely, no one was ever able to produce the

---

[40]*Supra*, note 10, at 112.
[41]*Ibid.*
[42]*Supra*, note 18, at 105.

body. There were several rumors about this at the time. One was that the body had been thrown into the Red River and had been carried away. The second was that Riel's men had badly mutilated the body and therefore were afraid to produce it.

There is, however, another version of the Scott affair which came to light recently when a statement made in 1938, by W. M. Joyce of Neepawa, Manitoba, was found in the Manitoba Archives by one of the Association's researchers.[43] Mr. Joyce relates a story told to him by a young Métis by the name of Fiddler. He was the son of a man who was an official member of Donald Smith's staff. According to this version, Scott, after his escape, went to the Lakehead where he worked as a labourer on the road construction which was taking place at the time. After a time, he returned to the Red River in February of 1870 to see a young woman friend. While there he was seen in the streets of Winnipeg by Riel's men who arrested him and returned him to prison. According to this version, the Fenian leader, O'Donoghue and several men came that night and spoke to Riel and his council. They then went to the prison where they released Scott. They took him with them on the agreement that he would, for a sum of money and the promise of a permanent job, go to the United States and never return to Canada. Fiddler says he travelled with them for about three miles and then went home. That was the last he had seen of Scott. The actual execution, he claims, was faked by one of O'Donoghue's men.

Whatever the truth of this affair, it is clear that the alleged execution of Scott played a major role in the reactions of the Canadian government to the Métis people in 1870. This event took place between the time the Red River delegates left for Ottawa and the time they arrived there. It resulted in their arrest and a great deal of pressure on the Macdonald government by the Ontario Orange Society to be punitive in its dealings with the Métis people.[44]

It has also been said by some who have studied the transcripts of Riel's trial, that this was the real reason for Riel's being found guilty and executed, rather than the high treason charge which was brought against him. In any event, Scott's execution, if indeed he was executed, plays a prominent role in the demise of Riel.

> The execution of Scott was a political mistake. But Riel could not

---

[43] W. M. Joyce, Manitoba Archives.
[44] *Supra*, note 9, at 72 and 75.

have foreseen that it would in the end cost him his life and that it would bedevil Canadian politics for half a century.[45]

> . . . In the years to come, both Scott and Riel ceased to be men, human beings with human frailties; they became political symbols, political slogans, around which men rallied and for which they argued and fought with little knowledge of the real strengths and weaknesses of the men whose names they bandied to and fro.
>
> By one unfortunate error of judgment — this is what the execution of Scott amounted to — and by one unnecessary deed of bloodshed — for the Provisional Government was an accomplished fact — Louis Riel set his foot upon the path which led not to glory but to the gibbet.[46]

E. THE PROMISED AMNESTY

One of the important requests or demands that the delegates carried with them was a demand that there be a guarantee of an amnesty for all persons who were in any way connected with the Red River Provisional Government.[47] Although Riel believed that he acted legally under the provisions of International Law, he recognized that the Canadian government had gone to great pains to avoid any official recognition of his government as the legitimate government of the people. Therefore, he suspected that the Canadian government would try to take punitive action against certain people once they gained legal control of the territory. He, therefore, wanted iron-clad assurance on the amnesty question. This issue, in fact, took precedence over the charter of rights and was the first one raised by Ritchot in the negotiations with Cartier and Macdonald.[48]

This issue had also been raised by Bishop Taché before his return to the Red River in the spring of 1870.

> Although he had known nothing of the Portage rising, and the shooting of Scott had yet to occur when Taché was in Ottawa, the Bishop sincerely believed that the promised amnesty included everything which had happened or might happen prior to his arrival in the Settlement. He had, in fact, raised this very question of bloodshed while talking with the Canadian ministers. For this reason he gave Riel and Lepine categorical assurances that an amnesty would be granted them covering all adventures and misadventures of the Red River rising. He told them, too, that they should go ahead with their plans to send a delegation to Ottawa and that the delegates would be well received by the Canadian authorities.[49]

Bishop Taché, therefore, operated on the belief that he had been

---

[45] *Ibid.*, at 69.
[46] *Supra*, note 10, at 117.
[47] W. L. Morton, *Manitoba: The Birth of a Province*, 1965, at 138.
[48] *Ibid.*
[49] *Supra*, note 10, at 121; Sessional Papers (No. 11) 38 Vic 1875 at 27.

promised a general amnesty by the authorities, but he never got anything official in writing to this effect.

In the negotiations in Ottawa, Macdonald took the position that the Canadian government could not grant such an amnesty because they had no legal authority in the territory during the period when the disturbances took place. Only the British government could grant such a request, they said. They did, however, promise to arrange a meeting with the British representative to discuss the matter. They implied that they would intervene in support of the request and saw no problem in making such an arrangement. A meeting was subsequently arranged with Sir Clinton Murdoch. Murdoch promised that a general amnesty would be arranged, declining however, to put the promise in writing despite the repeated requests by Ritchot. He claimed that it was not necessary since the amnesty could and would be arranged[50]

However, this promise was never kept. In spite of follow-up petitions by Bishop Taché and others to the British colonial office and to the Canadian government, the promised amnesty was not to become a reality for many years. In the meantime, warrants were issued for Riel and many of his followers, because of the Scott affair, alleging that they were guilty of murder. These warrants were sworn out by Scott's brother and were officially approved by none other than Donald Smith, who had been appointed as interim Lieutenant-Governor of the new territory until Archibald arrived in Manitoba.[51]

F. THE NEGLECT OF METIS RIGHTS OUTSIDE OF MANITOBA

Having resolved the Red River problems and gained legal control over all of Rupert's Land and the Northwest Territories from the British Crown, Macdonald operated on the assumption that the inhabitants outside of the Red River had no rights and that he did not need to deal with them. This is evidenced by a letter he wrote to Governor-General Lansdowne on August 12, 1884.

> Now these half-breeds have been told that they have the choice of going with father or mother as white men or they can get their homestead of 160 acres free on cultivation. If as Indians, they can join their mother's band and get their share of its reserve and of the annuities and presents secured to them by treaty.[52]

---

[50]*Supra,* note 47, at 146.
[51]*Supra,* note 8, at 83-84.
[52]*Supra,* note 9 at 131-132.

Sir John A. Macdonald — Prime Minister during both Métis disturbances at Red River and Batoche — From a photo in the Public Archives, Canada.

The Métis inhabitants, however, took a different view of the situation. In the belief that the people of the Red River had realized considerable success in their demands for the recognition of their rights, many of the rest of the Métis outside of the new province of Manitoba petitioned with requests for similar guarantees. There were a series of petitions from communities scattered throughout the Northwest, from Manitoba Village all the way to Edmonton. These petitions began in May, 1873, and continued until 1884.[53] As well, representatives were made by many church officials, government officials and members of the N.W.T Council on behalf of the Métis people.

The records show that these petitions were all passed on to Ottawa but the records show no official government response. Macdonald seems to have simply ignored these petitions. However, after being out of office for one term, the Conservatives were re-elected in 1878. Although not offically referring to the petitions, the government in an 1879 amendment to the *Dominion Land Acts*[54] made provisions for the extinguishment of the "Indian Title" of the half-breeds. Other than this legislative recognition, nothing more was done. In fact, as late as the 1885 session of Parliament, Macdonald denied that the Métis had any special rights. He stated that if the Métis wanted to be considered as Indians, they could join one of the Indian bands. If not, they could claim a homestead the same as any settler.[55] This was a consistent policy of his, as reflected in his letter, supra, to Lord Lansdowne. This continued to be the official position of the government until the beginning of the 1885 session of Parliament. By then it was obvious that there was further trouble in the Northwest. In a purported desperate attempt to head off the trouble, the Macdonald government finally began public action in March of 1885 to implement the "Indian Title" provisions of the *Dominion Land Act.*

G. EXPLOITATION OF THE METIS PEOPLE OF MANITOBA

The *Manitoba Act*[56] guaranteed a number of rights, among them being questions dealing with land. Those people settled on river lots

[53] *Sessional Papers* (No. 116) 48 Victoria 1884.
[54] 42 Vict., Chap. 31, s. 125(e).
[55] House of Commons Debates, Canada, May 4, 1885 at 1567.
[56] 33Victoria, Chapter 3.

were guaranteed that they would get their title to this property plus title to adjacent haylands that they had always used. The children of half-breed families were to be given land allocations in land reserves situated around the existing parishes. Originally no provisions were made for land grants to heads of families. This oversight, if indeed an oversight, was rectified by legislation in 1874, which made provision for such grants by issuance of scrip.[57]

It must be noted here, that when the Red River delegates asked for land rights, this was to be for all settlers, not just the Métis. The *Manitoba Act* basically dealt with the Métis. Later legislation granted similar land rights to the Selkirk settlers, the old settlers and their children.[58]

Before any action was taken on the land question, settlers began to flood into the Red River from the east. They often squatted on land claimed by Métis people or on land which they wanted included in the land reserves. In one example, at a place which became known as the Boyne River, the Métis returned from the hunt to find immigrants squatted on their land. The immigrants refused to move and a battle nearly resulted. Only Archibald's intervention prevented this from happening, by convincing the Métis to give up their claim in return for a promise of land away from the river.[59] There are other instances of Métis being forced off their land or being forced to sell by immigrants. The major exploitation, however, was by those who speculated in land. The research on what happened to Métis land in Manitoba is not complete. However, research that has been done indicates that most of the land grants to children passed into the hands of land speculators. In many cases land entitlements were sold long before they were distributed. There were a number of reasons for this, including the fact that it took ten years before the land allocations were complete. Many families were in immediate need. They sold for cash and moved further west where land was plentiful and where they could continue their traditional lifestyle.

One might assume that at least the riverlots would have stayed in Métis possession. Some did, but research shows that much of this land passed into the hands of various officials and speculators very quickly

---

[57]*An Act Respecting the Appropriation of Certain Dominion Lands in Manitoba*, 37 Victoria, Cap. 20, s.1.
[58]*Ibid.*
[59]*Supra*, note 18, at 165-166; also material from Manitoba Archives.

after 1870 and before the Métis had their title registered.[60] For example, research done on Manitoba parishes turned up the fact that Donald Smith acquired title to 10,000 acres in the parishes. Dr. John Schultz acquired 5,000 acres in these parishes. This is of considerable interest because the legislation did not provide for anyone but the occupants or those who had staked claims prior to July 15, 1870, to receive title to these riverlots. In addition, both Smith and Schultz were Members of Parliament representing Manitoba ridings at the time.

An *Order in Council*[61] also provided for the government to make blocks of land available to colonization companies for the purpose of assembling land and selling it to incoming settlers. These companies were usually formed by friends and allies of the Macdonald government and often included members of the government as shareholders. An example of such a land company was the Prince Albert Colonization Company. It included politicians such as White, Jamieson and Bowell.[62] Hugh Sutherland, also an M.P., was a trustee for this company. This particular company takes on significance because it was directly implicated in events which led to the Northwest Rebellion.

H. THE CONCERNS OF THE PEOPLE WHICH PROMPTED THEM TO ACT

As indicated above, the people had for many years been sending petitions to Ottawa in an attempt to get government action on their grievances with no results. The railway across Canada had now reached the prairies and settlers were beginning to come into the country in increasing numbers. Many of the Métis from Manitoba had settled in areas such as the Qu'Appelle Lakes, Maple Creek and St. Laurent. The St. Laurent community was one of the most active and best organized in the west. For example, it had adopted its own local laws known as the Laws of St. Laurent.[63] The origins of the community pre-dated the 1870 events in Manitoba. However, the community had seen a substantial migration of Métis families to the

---

[60] *Riverlots and Scrip, Elements of Métis Aboriginal Rights, 1978.*
[61] O.C., December 23, 1881.
[62] House of Commons Debates, Canada, April 5, 1886, at 488.
[63] *Documents and Articles about Métis People, 1972, Saskatchewan Archives,* Regina, at 42-48.

The Lindsay schoolhouse in the district of Lorne where the Métis and The Farmer's Union held their meetings — From a photo in the Saskatchewan Archives, Regina.

general area following 1870. The area had a number of other Métis communities including Fish Creek, Halcro, St. Louis and Duck Lake. In particular, there were settled in the area a number of Riel's lieutenants and supporters from the Red River. Most of these people were settled on riverlots in the pattern of the French survey system. They wanted these land-holdings guaranteed. A similar pattern of land-holdings had existed in various areas in the Qu'Appelle Valley, where, in spite of promises that title would be granted to riverlots, the surveyors decided to use the torrens survey system which crossed existing land-holdings and broke up many of these small farm-holdings.[64]

Given their previous experience in Manitoba plus the action on

[64]House of Commons Debates, Canada, June 1, 1886, at 1732 and in reply Mr. White, at 1733.

the Qu'Appelle, the residents on the South Saskatchewan began to fear for their land-holdings. The situation was further aggravated when the government assembled 36 townships of land for the Prince Albert Colonization Company.[65] This tract included much of the Métis land in the area of Batoche and St. Laurent. Before the deal with the company was finalized, six townships were withdrawn from the west side of the tract and six were added to the east side of the tract. The people naturally heard rumors about these transactions but they had no solid information about what was happening. The rumors became a reality for some people when the company attempted to evict settlers and the Catholic mission from the parish of St. Louis. This land remained within the limits of the land tract sold to the Company.

At this point the people, under the leadership of Gabriel Dumont, decided to take action to protect their interests. Dumont was well known among the plains Métis and Indians. He was a highly respected military leader and strategist. The native people were ready to support him in military action to protect their rights. Some urged him to initiate military action. Dumont, however, was not satisfied that all legal efforts had been exhausted. He understood the situation required a charismatic person to carry on potential negotiations and to help unite the people. It was also believed at the time that many of the white settlers would support the Métis cause, due to the widespread dissatisfaction in the west with regard to government policy. This was especially so in the Prince Albert area. They had been promised the mainline railway through their area. Not only did they not get the railway, but were faced as well with high overland freight costs and no market outlet for their farm produce.

Dumont and his supporters discussed the possibility of bringing Riel back to lead his people. It was agreed that an attempt should be made. A delegation was sent to visit him and explain the situation, as well as to request his leadership.

I. RIEL RETURNS

The story of Riel's return has been popularized in books, movies and in other ways. Therefore, it is not necessary to repeat all of the

---

[65]*Supra*, note 62, at 488-489.

details here. Riel by this time was an American citizen. This, coupled with his experience in Manitoba and his abortive attempts to take a seat in the House of Commons, made him reluctant to consider the offer. Besides, he and his wife and children had to live and the position offered him provided no compensation. Nevertheless, he was finally convinced that he should return and did so with the delegation. They arrived at Batoche around the end of June, 1884. As Riel arrived, he was met by a large gathering of people. Messengers were subsequently dispatched to inform all the halfbreeds — English as well as French — that Riel would address them the next day. The meeting took place at the parish church. Recognizing the anguish and excitement of the people, Riel attempted to quiet their anxiety with the following words:

> It is useless to feel so much grief. If we conduct ourselves openly, methodically and persistently, it is impossible for the government not to see the justice of our requests and satisfy them. Patience and calm and the use of all constitutional means at your disposal are the best way to achieve desired results. That is how we acted at the Red River. Therefore, continue your petitions.[66]

Several days later he addressed a large crowd of people in Prince Albert. He took a similar moderate tone in his speech at this gathering. A number of people including William Jackson, of the Settler's Union, spoke in his support. A fund was organized to provide resources for Riel whom they named "The National Advocate".

That Riel was not the wide-eyed radical and agitator who returned to stir up the people against the government is bolstered by, amongst others, Father André. André wrote letters on July 7 and July 21, 1884, to Lieutenant-Governor Dewdney informing him of Riel's constitutional agitation, as opposed to danger of armed insurrection.

> You know that I am known to be a friend of Mr. Riel and I looked to the event of his arrival among us as danger for the peace of our community, but now I do not entertain the least suspicion about Riel causing any trouble. He acts quietly and speaks wisely . . .
>
> . . . All his endeavors, as far as I know, are to make the people understand that in answering their call he had in view no other object than to help them by legitimate and peaceful means . . .[67]

J. EVENTS LEADING TO THE REBELLION

Following Riel's return and at his urging, petition after petition

---

[66] *Supra,* note 8, at 102.

[67] *Supra,* note 9, at 128.

was dispatched to Ottawa pressing the government for some action on Métis demands. Many meetings were held during the summer at which the people resolved to persevere in their efforts to win their rights. Nothing happened. The government did not respond.

In the early fall they drew up a list of rights as had been done at the Red River. This was then sent to Ottawa with a petition asking for guarantees. The Charter contained seven clauses:

1. Subdivision of the Northwest Territories into Provinces.
2. Concessions of land and other advantages to the Métis, similar to those granted to their Manitoba brothers.
3. Immediate distribution of land titles to settlers in possession.
4. Sale of a half-million acres of Crown lands for the foundation of schools, hospitals, and other institutions of this kind in Métis settlements, and for furnishing seed grain and farm implements for poor Métis.
5. The reservation of 100 districts of marshy land to be distributed among Métis children in the course of the next 120 years.
6. Allocation of $1,000 to maintain a religious institution in each Métis settlement.
7. Arrangements for Indian well-being.[68]

Ottawa ignored this petition as well. Meetings continued, more petitions were signed and sent to Ottawa. Still no official response from Ottawa. Unofficially, a Mr. Reney and Joseph Forget, claiming to be Senators, offered Riel a seat on the Northwest Council, saying that this would give him a chance to redress their grievances. No one took this proposal seriously.[69] With all this government inaction, by mid-winter of 1885 Riel decided that his presence might be militating against the people's interest. He suggested that it might be to their advantage if he returned to Montana. The people refused to hear of this and were unanimous that they were prepared to fight if Riel remained as their leader. Riel agreed to stay.[70]

[68] *Supra*, note 8, at 103.
[69] *Ibid.*
[70] *Ibid., at 104-105.*

V.

THE NORTHWEST REBELLION

A. THE DECISION TO RESIST GOVERNMENT TYRANNY

During the course of these meetings, the Canadian officials were making plans for the enforcement of their authority in the troubled area. Of course, their answer was the use of force.[71] During the build-up of this armed force, around the 18th of March, 1885, a Hudson's Bay factor, Lawrence Clarke, on his return from Winnipeg, met a group of Métis and stated to them, upon their answer that they were still holding meetings:

> . . . Ah, you are still holding meetings. And Riel and Dumont are leading you! Well, 500 policemen are on the way here to keep them quiet. In answer to your requests, they have chains for Riel and bullets for the members of his council. You will soon have news of them. I met them at Humboldt.[72]

This news spurred the Métis into action. They formed a Provisional Government and through known government spies in their ranks, Riel dispatched a letter to Major Crozier of the Mounted Police, asking that the forts at Carleton and North Battleford be turned over to the Provisional Government. Riel also made it known to the government, through these spies, that the Métis had resolved to fight for the realization of their rights if necessary.

Crozier's response was to demand the surrender of the Métis leaders and the dispersal of the armed men. Nothing further happened until March 25, when a troop of Mounted Police appeared on the banks of the South Saskatchewan opposite Batoche. This action by the Police spurred Dumont into action. He decided to get more arms and ammunition, as well as supplies for his men. A military council was formed and a troop dispatched to Duck Lake, under Dumont, to

[71] *Supra*, note 18, at 321; *Supra*, note 9, at 133.
[72] *Supra*, note 8, at 104; *Supra*, note 10, at 305.

seize arms and goods from the store of Hilliard Mitchell, who was one of the government spies.

B. THE DUCK LAKE AFFAIR

Dumont proceeded to Duck Lake with 30 men and helped himself to the provisions in Mitchell's store. As they were returning to their horses, several horsemen rode by, warning of the approach of the Police and then fled. One of these men was recognized as Thomas McKay, another government spy. Dumont and two of his men chased them, but stopped when they saw about 22 police. They then returned to Duck Lake and had just stabled their horses, when the cry of police

A drawing depicting the battle between the Métis and the North West Mounted Police at Duck Lake in March, 1885 — From a filmstrip on the 1885 uprising, by Charlebois.

came again. This time Crozier appeared with 177 men under his command. Dumont, having only 30 men, ordered them to take positions on a hill overlooking the road.

There are several versions of what happened next. In any event, because Riel had instructed him not to fire first if he encountered the police, Gabriel sent peace emissaries to converse with Crozier. According to Tremaudan, McKay shot Isadore Dumont, Gabriel's brother, as they approached the police force. This was followed by Crozier's orders to open fire, killing the Indian, Assywin.[73]

However, according to Charlebois, Isadore Dumont and Assywin, carrying a white flag, met Crozier and McKay. McKay, in an interview with the Daily Herald, which was published 50 years later, admitted that he drew his pistol and shot Assywin and immediately after this murder, shot and killed Dumont.[74]

A full-scale battle ensued which lasted about 30 minutes. Riel arrived during the battle with reinforcements. After the height of the battle, Crozier and his men began to retreat. Riel gave orders that they be allowed to do so and forbade his men to chase them. The retreating police left twelve dead and one wounded behind. They also left arms, ammunition and other supplies. The Métis lost five men.

Crozier, on his arrival at Fort Carleton, decided to destroy the fort and supplies and retreat to Prince Albert, which was in a better defensible situation. Riel, also, forbade his men to ambush Crozier and his men on their way to Prince Albert. He further refused to sanction any attacks on the police and militia who had barricaded themselves in Prince Albert. Instead, Riel concentrated on preparing for the expected military and police expedition they believed was coming from the south. They seized further arms and supplies at Duck Lake and at Clarke's Crossing on the South Saskatchewan. They built a system of defence trenches at Batoche and, in general, prepared themselves for the skirmish with Middleton who was now on the way to Batoche. Dumont again suggested that a guerrilla action be launched against Middleton's troops en route to Batoche. They could harrass and tire them, thereby reducing their numbers before they arrived. Again Riel refused to approve such tactics which he felt were too barbarous. Riel still seemed to entertain the notion that somehow the

---

[73]*Ibid.*, at 107.
[74]*Supra*, note 9, at 148.

battle could be avoided and the grievances settled peacefully. He, in particular, abhorred the thought of using Indian war tactics. He considered the tactics to be uncivilized. Dumont submitted to Riel's wish and returned to Batoche with his men, where he awaited Middleton.

General Middleton, a British career soldier, at the head of 5000 regular and volunteer troops on march to Batoche — From a photo in the Public Archives, Canada.

C. MIDDLETON'S EXPEDITION

Sir John A. Macdonald, as soon as he heard of the battle at Duck Lake, authorized military action. In preparation for possible trouble General Middleton had been dispatched to Winnipeg on March 23, 1885. The 90th battalion and the Winnipeg Field Battery were mobilized. On March 26, the day following the Duck Lake battle, those troops under Middleton's command left Winnipeg for

Qu'Appelle by train. Here they disembarked and began the trip to Batoche on horseback. By April 16, Middleton and his men were within 30 miles of Clarke's Crossing on the South Saskatchewan. The Federal government, which had ignored the Métis petitions for more than ten years — partly because they did not want to spend the money that would have been involved in meeting the demands — in a matter of three weeks, at a cost of millions of dollars, had now mobilized an army and moved it to what was to become a battlefield.

At the same time, the government in Ottawa decided to act on the long-neglected grievances and petitions. An Order in Council was approved quickly by cabinet to implement the provisions contained in *the Dominion Land Act.*[75] By March 31, a commission had been established to go to the West and deal with M*étis grievances and to settle the land question.*

D. THE METIS DEFENCE

The Métis made their first defence at Fish Creek about 12 miles to the south of St. Laurent. Dumont, with 150 men under his command, met Middleton who was leading 1,000 men. Fifty more men were left under Riel's command to confront an approaching Mounted Police detachment from Qu'Appelle. Dumont, meanwhile, deployed his men in a deep hollow by Fish Creek. A battle began on April 24 and ended on April 25, when Dumont decided to retreat to the Batoche defences. The Métis had four casualties; Middleton had a total of sixty — ten dead and fifty wounded.

Middleton next decided to attack the Métis defences at Batoche, both by land and from the river. One hundred and eight men were sent on the steamer Northcote, toward the settlement, equipped with a gattling gun. This attempted assault from the steamboat took place on May 9, 1885. Meanwhile, Middleton was moving a large infantry troop toward Batoche. The Métis, by stringing a cable across the river, disabled the Northcote and it drifted downstream about three miles where it lay useless. Neither the boat nor its troops played any part in the battle. Although the Métis had built a good defence system around Batoche, they were poorly armed and had very little ammunition, their guns mostly buffalo guns.

---

[75]O.C., March 30, 1885.

The Metis defenses at Batoche — From a photo in the Saskatchewan Archives, Regina.

Middleton's troops on the other hand were armed with the latest army issue rifles. They had a large supply of ammunition, and in addition, a gattling gun. The battle at Batoche began May 9, 1885. The surrender took place five days later on May 13, 1885. Although Dumont and his men fought valiantly, they were no match for the overwhelming and well-armed force under Middleton. The Métis morale was also badly shaken when the priests at Batoche refused to continue to extend religious services to the men. Riel himself did not bear arms in the fight. He spent most of his time going about the trenches, bolstering the morale of the men and reading to them from the Bible.

Riel, through the auspices of a surveyor named Astley, also carried on negotiations with Middleton concerning safety of the women and children who were being sheltered in the village church. Arrangements were made for them to be placed in a building under a white flag which Middleton promised not to fire upon. Negotiations were also conducted for the safety of the prisoners which the Métis held. After a concerted attack by Middleton's men on May 12, the Métis were finally forced to abandon their trenches and retreat to the village. They continued for awhile to hold off the soldiers from a piece of rising ground. By May 13, the battlefield was quiet. The decision was made to surrender. The Métis went in small groups to submit themselves to the victors. They were always preceded by white flags. Some went alone; some went in the company of their priests.

Dumont, Nault, Dumas and several other key members of the groups escaped into the bush and eventually made their way to Montana. As described earlier in this submission, Riel surrendered peaceably to the scouts who delivered him to Middleton. The Northwest Rebellion was now over. The casualties included 51 Métis dead and 73 wounded, out of a total of approximately 300 Métis who had been under arms.[76]

E. THE AFTERMATH

The rebellion itself and the events which followed stirred up strong feelings. The Ontario Orangemen and those Orangemen who had moved west were intent on revenge. Macdonald, as well, wanted revenge against Riel, although in parliamentary debates, he pretended to maintain a moderate approach, saying the courts would decide the guilt or innocence of Riel. In private, however, Macdonald said of the amnesty recommendation by the jury and the pressure for a reprieve for Riel from Quebec that, "Riel shall hang though every dog in Quebec shall bay."[77] The eastern-controlled Orange newspapers screamed for Riel's head. It is doubtful that Riel could have received a fair trial anywhere outside Quebec.

In spite of the highly inflammatory voices that were raised against Riel, there were others more familiar with the situation who spoke out much more objectively about the events. Major Walsh of the N.W.M.P., for example, who had spent much of his time among

---

[76]The information contained in the preceding pages was obtained from Tremaudan's book. This information is heavily relied upon, as it was initiated by our own people.
[77]*Supra,* note 9, at 232.

Drawing depicting the capture of Riel by N.W.M.P. scouts — From a photo in the Saskatchewan Archives, Regina.

the Indians and Métis, wrote as follows when he heard about the rebellion:

> When the first news of the Métis rising reached me, I couldn't believe, and I still can't believe that they want war . . . I think a commission should have been established long ago. However, the fact that this was neglected is no reason why it should not be set up and sent without further delay. What glory for Canada lies in killing a few poor Métis who find themselves neglected? Don't forget that these people have the heartfelt sympathy of all the white inhabitants of the area. Do you imagine that if the whites had the same grievances as the Métis they wouldn't rebel? And if they did, is there a single man in Canada who would oppose setting up a commission? These people aren't rebels; they are simply asking for justice.[78]

Riel's trial was a political trial. He was not only accused as the

[78]R.C.M.P. Correspondence, from R.C.M.P. Archives, Regina.

perpetrator of the uprising at Batoche; during the trial, Crown lawyers also pictured him as a bloodthirsty villain who was responsible for actions at Cutknife, North Battleford and Frog Lake.[79] The uprising at Batoche was followed by a number of similar actions by Indian tribes in the Northwest who were starving and who had their own grievances with the government. According to Father Scollen, R.C.:

> The Métis insurrection had not necessarily been the cause of the Indian uprising; the Indians had been ready to revolt long before the Métis rebelled. They were ready to seize the first opportunity that presented itself — and that's what they did. If other people had had difficulties with the Government or had caused trouble, the Indians would have acted in the same way.[80]

It is true that Dumont had contacts with the chiefs of these tribes and they knew of the Métis actions to get justice from Ottawa for themselves and for the Indian people. However, they had not been incited to rebellion by Riel; they had in fact been restrained by him from rebelling earlier in the fall of 1884. It was only when news of the action at Batoche reached Big Bear and other chiefs that they started their own actions. These were based on their own decisions and were not directly influenced by Riel. The main concern of the Indians was the lack of wildlife to subsist upon and the threat of starvation. Not only was wildlife getting scarce, but the Indians were forced upon their reserves. As Macdonald pointed out in the Commons:

> . . . We kept them on short rations, on short allowances, and we tried to force them — I am speaking of the Indians — and we have forced them upon their reserves;[81]

Riel was also pictured at the trial as having returned to Canada from Montana for the explicit purpose of starting the rebellion. Nothing could be further from the truth. Riel did everything in his power to avoid bloodshed, encouraging the people to use legitimate means to gain their rights. As outlined earlier in this submission, the records clearly support this view. Father André in a letter to Dewdney following the events at Batoche remarked that, "A man doesn't take his wife and children with him if he intends to stir up a revolt."

The actions of Riel do not bear out the accusations that later followed his voluntary capture. As illustrated earlier, the Battle of Duck Lake was largely accidental and could have been avoided by

---

[79] *Supra*, note 3, at 337-343.
[80] *Supra*, note 8, at 116.
[81] House of Commons Debates, March 26, 1886, at 762.

Major Crozier. Riel's sparing of Crozier and his men's lives surely is not consistent with a blood-thirsty man. His refusal to allow guerrilla tactics against General Middleton's main troop does not portray wanton disregard for other people's lives, but reflects his desire to reach a peaceful solution to their legitimate grievances.

VI.

The Government Responsibility

A. GOVERNMENT CONFUSION AND INDECISION

What is quite clear from our study of historical records, including our examination of the most biased accounts, is that the government of Canada was responsible for the trouble both at the Red River and more particularly at Batoche. It was the arrogant assumption by the government of Canada in 1869 that the territory of Rupert's Land and the Northwest Territories were theirs, which led to their disregard of the Métis people and their rights. When the inhabitants of the area objected, Macdonald saw this as a challenge to Canadian authority and the resistance of the people as a rebellion to be put down. Macdonald only agreed to negotiate with the people because he saw that as being cheaper than carrying out military action. He tried to buy off the leaders (Riel in particular) but this failed. Macdonald negotiated in bad faith and as he said in a letter to Rose, once the government achieved its objective of joining the area with Canada, he would swamp the Métis with immigration.[82]

Having dealt with the people of Red River, he saw no need to deal with the grievances of the people outside Manitoba. As indicated earlier, Macdonald consistently took the position that the Métis had no rights, that they could choose to be either settlers, white or Indians. As settlers, they could file for a homestead like any immigrant coming to the area. If they wanted special rights they should join an Indian band. In correspondence he referred to the Métis as miserable dogs, spoilt, etc., clearly showing his contempt for them and for their rights.[83] In public he managed to manipulate the political situation to make it appear that he was a moderate understanding man, but that he

---

[82]*Supra*, note 9, at 114.

[83]Macdonald Papers, Public Archives of Canada, one example being a letter to Rose, February 23, 1870.

had to deal with and compromise with the reality of the powerful Ontario Orangemen. The Orangemen who were certainly powerful, vengeful and racist became nevertheless scapegoats of Macdonald.

In spite of the repeated petitions from people over a ten-year period, the government did nothing. They did not even respond to most of the petitions. This course of action or inaction was followed even though the amendment in 1879 to the *Dominion Land Act* provided for the extinguishment of the half-breed's right to Indian title in the Northwest Territories.

> Only under pressure of an outbreak did the government take action. A judicial inquiry, under C. B. Rouleau, was finally sent out to investigate the claims of the half-breeds; Rouleau reported that "the report concerning the Indians' and half-breeds' claims should be settled under the shortest possible delay because the agitation may become very serious . . . there will be great misery and starvation this winter. . .
>
> . . .
>
> The total cost of the Rebellion amounted to over 5 million dollars. This was a far cry from the $74,121.33 that the government had "saved" in 1884 with the policy of reduced expenditure in the Northwest. . .
>
> . . .
>
> The federal government in Ottawa must bear the greatest share of the responsibility for the rebellion, for reports from Dewdney and others provided important information and alarming facts all during 1884. Macdonald was made fully aware of the problems of settlers, Métis and Indians, but nothing was done to ease the situation. Instead, Macdonald had taken the view that "no amount of concession will prevent people from grumbling and agitating. . ." The French-English strife which was to divide Canada in the future was the most tragic legacy of the rebellion. For this, the government alone was to blame for its lack of true understanding of the serious nature of the rebellion.[84]

As noted from the above reference, the government in 1884 received from various sources, information of the seriousness of the Métis constitutional agitation, as well as the general state of starvation. However, prior to this period, the government was poorly advised by its senior government officials in the area. The vengeful Hayter Reed, Assistant Indian Commissioner, saw the native people as an uncivilized bunch of savages to be dealt with severely and punitively. He was constantly urging punitive action and restrictive and racist policies on the government. His memorandum of 1885, in which he urged a number of punitive actions against the Indians and

---

[84]Taken from an autobiography of Edgar Dewdney contained in the Glenbow-Alberta Institute.

Métis involved in the rebellion, was typical of his stance.[85] It is of more than passing interest that the Macdonald government incorporated many of Reed's recommendations into an Order-in-Council. Some, such as the pass system for Indians on reserves, remained part of government policy until 1951.

That Hayter Reed was a complete despot and bigot is borne out by Captain Deane of the North West Mounted Police. According to Deane, when Lieutenant-Governor Dewdney was out of the territories in 1884, Reed was in charge and "his word was law".[86] Deane gives a vivid description of the starving Indians at Crooked Lake and of Reed's policy. He also mentions that his references to the Crooked Lake incident dealing with starvation in his report were struck out by Reed before being forwarded to his superiors.[87] He further states that this incident did not come to public knowledge until three and a half years later through an editorial in the Edmonton Bulletin, October, 1887.[88] That conditions for Indian people in the Northwest in the early and mid-1880's were less than human are borne out by such statements of Captain Deane, as well as references in other source material.

Edgar Dewdney, Lieutenant-Governor of the Northwest and Indian Commissioner, was possibly more tolerant toward the native people, but nevertheless, was a strong advocate of not recognizing Métis rights. However, for the most part he misled Macdonald into believing that everything in the Northwest was under control and that the government need pay no attention to the petitions and other signs of trouble. When he did finally begin to express concern in 1884 about the state of affairs in the Northwest, Macdonald at first ignored his warnings and his recommendation on remedial government action. It was not until March 1885 that Macdonald was convinced that the government should act to implement the provisions of the 1879 *Dominion Land Act*. However, even that limited response to Métis petitions was never communicated to the Métis. If it had been, it is likely that Riel would have been able to restrain the Métis force at Batoche, while he attempted further negotiations.

---

[85]Dewdney Papers, Glenbow-Alberta Institute.

[86]Deane, *Mounted Police Life in Canada*, 1916, at 140.

[87]*Ibid.*, at 149.

[88]*Ibid.*, at 149-150.

Edgar Dewdney, Lieutenant-Governor of the Northwest Territories at the time of the 1885 Uprising — From a photo in ***History of Regina.***

Instead, the government offered Riel a bribe to leave the country.[89], spread rumors of impending police action against the Métis, spread a rumor that an army was on the way and in other ways acted to incite the Métis and make the situation worse. For example, William Pearce who was sent out in 1884 to inquire into the riverlot claims on the South Saskatchewan, did not follow through with his task in an effective manner. There was ample evidence of the half-breeds' desire to acquire title of their riverlots by the form of letters and petitions to the government. Pearce, however, was not knowledgeable of the French language and did not pursue his mission in any sort of reasonable manner.[90] He merely stated that the majority of the residents were from Manitoba and had received land grants there. As a consequence no action was taken to reconcile this problem.

To add to the problem, as mentioned earlier, the Prince Albert Colonization Company had been granted a large tract of land which encompassed the area that Pearce was to investigate. Although the residents were anxious about this situation, local government officials were assuring them that they would get their title to the riverlots. However, the company's attempt to clear some of them from the tract provoked more than mere written requests.

Pearce again was sent into the area after the Rebellion for the purposes of whitewashing the government's inciting of the half-breeds' resistance to eviction by the company. Pearce, along with a half-breed interpreter, tricked the people into signing affidavits to the effect that they knew nothing about the Land Company before the Rebellion. This, however, was shortly discovered; a new testimonial was written out, exposing the treachery of Pearce and the government in its attempt to exonerate itself from responsibility for fomenting armed resistance.[91]

It is also interesting to note, especially in view of the numerous assertions of hard times in the Northwest that the Government action against the Métis helped to save the economy and expose the territory to prospective settlers.

---

[89]At the trial, the government's attempt to bribe Riel was made to appear as another by Riel to sell out the cause.

[90]Devrome, *The Metis, 1821-1885,* 1976, at 165.

[91]House of Commons Debates, Canada, June 1, 1886, at 1737.

> With the outbreak of the Rebellion in 1885 every farmer who owned, or could provide himself with a team of horses and a wagon, could hire himself out to the Government at ten dollars per day. Money poured into the country to feed and supply the troops and police. Militia officers and men visited the country on service when otherwise they would never have thought of coming so far west, and the Northwest Territories and their possibilities thus became widely known. In short, the Rebellion saved the country which, as an eastern correspondent wrote to me in 1884, "was not what it had been cracked up to be."[92]

Not only was the economy stimulated, which placated the white settlers and farmers, but the great railroad dream of John A. Macdonald about to be shattered, was resurrected. When the news of the police agression at Duck Lake was received, Prime Minister Macdonald used the half-breeds as a scapegoat to realize his C.P.R. dream, a small price as far as he was concerned, as opposed to uniting British Columbia to the east, along with the potential votes.

> We can only guess how long it took for the drink-sodden but wily mind of Sir John A. Macdonald to realize that if he magnified this skirmish into major proportions, presenting these relatively minor troubles to the Canadian public as a major rebellion and Indian uprising, he could scare Parliament into advancing money to complete the C.P.R. for the immediate transfer of troops and supplies to the Northwest.
>
> Months later Macdonald admitted that he had committed this almost unbelievable act of political opportunism.[93]

B. THE POLITICAL TRIAL

1. Pre-trial Politics

Although there were many factors involved in the 1885 Rebellion —amongst others, the economy and C.P.R. — the government was also acutely aware of the great discontent prevalent amongst all the inhabitants of the Northwest, both native and non-native. The Northwest was still not heavily populated and the threats of American annexation were still fresh in the government's mind.

The trial of Riel following the Resistance and his subsequent surrender was permeated by political decisions. The first political move, as outlined earlier, was the directive to have Riel transported to Regina as opposed to Winnipeg. This, of course, denied Riel the inviolable right to a jury composed of twelve of his peers. As such, French or half-breed Catholics could have been empanelled. Riel

---

[92]Supra, note 86, at 183.

[93]*Supra,* note 9, at 147.

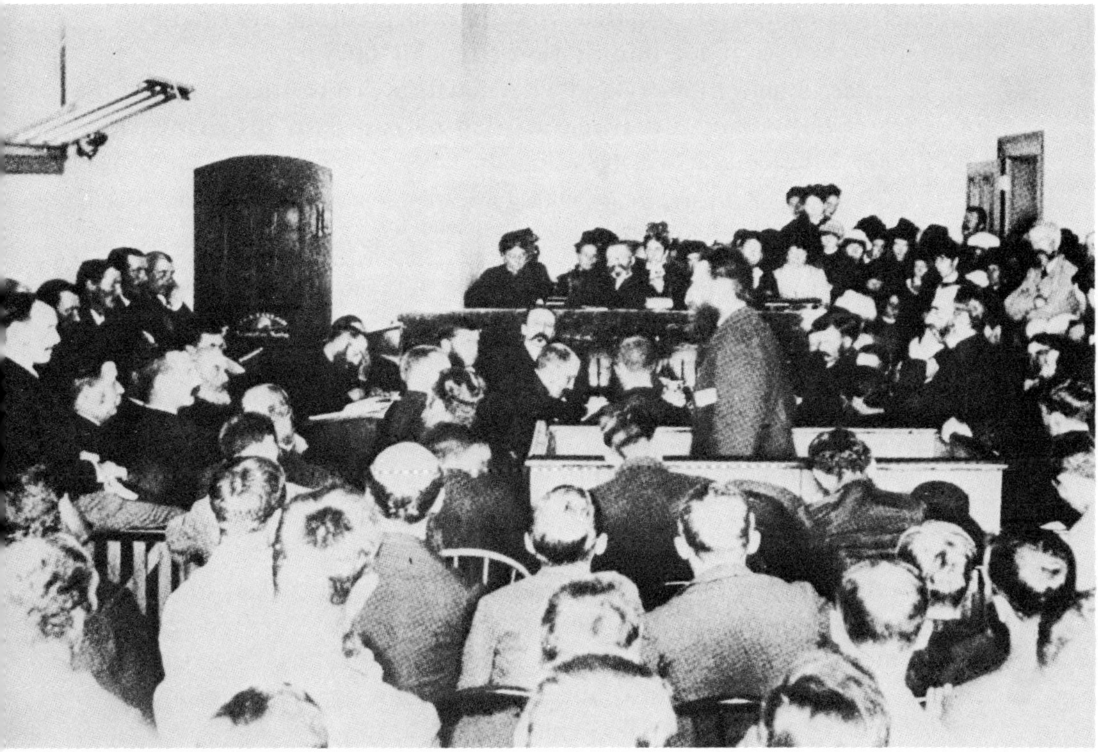

A picture of the trial of Riel — From a photo in the Saskatchewan Archives, Regina.

would also have been allowed the right under Manitoba law to have his trial conducted in the French language.

Riel's arrival at Regina was also greeted by another political decision. He was placed in the hands of Captain Deane, who decided that no one could have access to Riel without permission from the government.

> In reporting his arrival to the Police Department at Ottawa, I said that I intended to allow no visitor to have speech of the prisoner without a permit from the Prime Minister. I religiously held to this regulation of my own making and it saved me a great deal of trouble.[94]

Riel was also denied the opportunity to read any material that dealt with the resistance or any current affairs relating to it.[95] As well he would later only be allowed visitors who were given a permit by

---

[94]*Supra,* note 86, at 185.

[95]*Ibid.,* at 186.

Robinson, the Chief Crown Prosecutor.[96] It would therefore appear that Riel was completely isolated from knowledge of the aftermath of the resistance, except for information from his lawyers.

In order to better understand what constitutes a political trial the following excerpts from an article written by Assistant Professor of Law, Peter MacKinnon will be utilized:

> . . . A trial tends to be political when those in government feel directly threatened by the actions of the defendants.
>
> . . .
>
> . . . But in times of political turmoil or crisis, the distinction between "legal" and "political" issues becomes blurred.
>
> . . .
>
> . . . Leaders or spokesmen are readily identified as promoters and agitators who have provoked their normally peaceful and contented followers to serve their own ends. The suggestion that wide-spread protest could, in fact, be a spontaneous movement would reflect adversely on the well-being of people and thereby on the quality of their government.[97]

From the preceding portion of this submission it is clear that the events surrounding the Métis, Riel and the Northwest Territories as a whole, met the criteria for the ingredients of a political trial. The noted author, Joseph Howard, also adverts to treason as being a political matter and concludes that Riel's trial reeked of politics.

> Treason, as distinct from any other crime, is an offense against the current political regime of the state and the regime therefore becomes an intensely interested party to the proceeding — not as agent for the social community, as in its own right. Acquittal of a treason defendant is an implicit repudiation of the policies of the ruling regime.
>
> There can be little question that the circumstances of Louis Riel's trial were immoral. Whether the trial itself was also illegal has been debated ever since it was held.[98]

That the white population, at least around Batoche and area, supported and contributed to the political and constitutional agitation of Riel and the Council has been pointed out.[99] This, of necessity, would be adverse to the government's political interests and popularity. The government, therefore, had to adopt measures which would satisfy the settlers; otherwise their continued support of the

---

[96] *Ibid.*

[97] Peter MacKinnon. "Conspiracy and Sedition as Canadian Political Crimes," 1977, 23 *McGill Law Journal* 622, at 622-623.

[98] *Supra*, note 7, at 508.

[99] *Supra*, note 10, at 270 and 272. The French half-breeds supported the Settler's Union and English half-breeds because their grievances in regards to land and title were substantially the same.

Métis cause and discontent with government policy would be a testimonial reflecting the government's poor administration in the area. Macdonald, however, was willing to sit back for awhile longer and, fortunately for himself, the Duck Lake incident relieved him of considering white armed support for the Métis. At a meeting on March 22, 1885, the English settlers and English half-breeds decided that they would continue to sympathize with the Métis cause, but that they would remain neutral as to armed resistance.[100] Macdonald could now send in his army without fear of complete territorial resistance and deal with political implications later.

Macdonald, as pointed out on page 70 supra, took advantage of the unfortunate Duck Lake incident to forward his own political objectives and career. He immediately received money from Parliament to suppress the "Rebellion" and for the completion of the "National Dream" which resulted in a nightmare for the Métis.

After perpetrating this outlandish and bloody piece of opportunism, Macdonald, after Riel's sentence of execution for high treason was rendered, had the audacity to write that the incident lacked political overtones and that it should only be classified as a "mere domestic disturbance". The basis for this is contained in a letter of August 28, 1885, written to Governor-General Lansdowne:

> Your Excellency draws a distinction between treason as having a political aspect, and other crimes. Now there are treasons and treasons — any armed resistance to the Queen's authority is technically treason, but may have no political significance. If there were any international complications likely to arise with the United States, the distinction would be obvious.
>
> . . . .
>
> But this Northwest outbreak was a mere domestic trouble, and ought not to be elevated to the rank of a rebellion.
>
> The offences of Riel were riot and murder of such an extensive nature as to make them technically amount to treason . . .[101]

Lansdowne, however, was bright enough to realize and admit that the Government, having taken advantage of the situation, could not now down-play the seriousness of the action embarked upon. He replied to Macdonald's letter on August 31, 1885, disagreeing that the resistance could now be classified as "a mere domestic trouble".

> The outbreak was, no doubt, confined to our own territory and may therefore properly be described as a domestic trouble, but I am afraid we

---

[100] *Ibid.*, at 312.
[101] *Supra*, note 9, 229.

> have all of us been doing what we could to elevate it to the rank of a rebellion, and with so much success that we cannot now reduce it to the rank of a common riot.
>
> If the movement had been at once stamped out by the N.W.M.P., the case would have been different, but we were within an ace of an Indian war; the progress of the outbreak and its suppression has been described in glowing language by the press all over the world; we brought up troops from all parts of the Dominion; those troops have been thanked by Parliament; they are to receive an Imperial medal.[102]

Macdonald, finding no quarter in that area, nevertheless makes it clear in his reply on September 3, 1885, that the political implications of the cause of the resistance and the subsequent trial should not be admitted.

> I fear that you *have me* with respect to the charter given the outbreak. We have certainly made it assume large proportions in the public eye. This has been done, however, *for our own purposes,* and, I think, wisely done.
>
> What I ventured to suggest in my letter was that the persons convicted in Regina, should be convicted of municipal and not political offences.[103]

From the tone of these letters it is apparent that Macdonald had been resolved not to act on the jury's recommendation of clemency. As long as he could convince himself that the matter did not have political overtones, it would not warrant the Queen's mercy. The letters to Lansdowne, however, reeked of politics. The one of August 28, 1885, reflects Macdonald's analysis of the situation in terms of potential votes. He states that any appearance of desire on the part of the Government to facilitate an appeal to England would have "far-reaching consequences of a disastrous character", as the English-speaking people of Canada had strong feelings on this subject. He further wrote that the French in Quebec will not totally support Riel and revival of patriotic feelings will not extend far.

No doubt, Macdonald was quite aware of the strong feelings of the Orange Lodge and the expected reaction from them if an appeal was launched. In fact, when the press reported that an appeal against the conviction was set in motion, the Orangemen reacted vehemently.

> Orange Lodges in their meetings resolved to send demands that Riel be hanged. "We submit that it is the duty of the government," said the

---

[102]*Ibid.*

[103]Ibid., at 230.

Orange Sentinel, "to take no account of the recommendation for clemency, but to let this law take its course in the interest of the Dominion in general . . . He committed a most infamous and most atrocious murder against a loyal Protestant subject."[104]

Not surprisingly, Macdonald himself later admitted that he believed Riel to be a murderer of Scott and definitely placed himself in a position of bias, which most certainly had influenced the prosecution and conviction of Riel. Although he was adverting to the 1870 incident, the following remarks by Macdonald made in Parliament on March 26, 1885, certainly reflected his attitude toward Riel.

The man who was shot, Thomas Scott, was of Irish origin . . . $5,000 was offered for this traitor and murderer, . . . We have got a special statute, under which such criminals can be tried, and he would have been tried *and found guilty.*[105]

Four days after Riel's execution, Macdonald wrote to Dewdney, Lieutenant-Governor, Northwest Territories, expressing his hope that the execution would have a good effect on the half-breeds and the scheduled hanging of 27 Indians would convince the Redman who is boss.[106] Undoubtedly, the decision not to extend clemency to Riel was to serve as an example to the Métis that they were at the mercy of the government; and that if they didn't co-operate they could expect similar treatment.

That Riel was to be used as the example of government might is indicated by the fact that only he was charged with high treason. The others were charged with lesser offences which could be served in jail. This, of course, was another political decision as the prosecution, a member of which was the Junior Minister of Justice, no doubt received instructions as to their manner of approach which was to place "all the responsibility for the uprising on Riel".[107]

According to Garnot, a member of the Provisional Government, in writing about his imprisonment in Regina jail;

One day, they (prosecuting lawyers) came and called us (Metis councillors) all together and explained to us the difference between the charge of high treason, for which we should infallibly suffer sentence of death, and that of treason-felony, for which we could suffer imprisonment of from one day to life . . .

They then told us, "We have decided to condemn you, and we see no

---

[104]*Ibid.*, at 230-231.

[105]House of Commons Debates, Canada, March 26, 1885, at 764-765. (Emphasis added)

[106]Letter of November 10, 1885, Dewdney Papers, Glenbow Alberta Institute.

[107]*Supra,* note 9, at 220; See also, *Supra,* note 10, at 342.

Hugh Richardson, Stipendiary Magistrate, before whom Riel was arraigned, convicted and sentenced to hang. Photo from ***The Northwest Rebellion*** *— Nick and Helma Mika.*

means to save you, *for you certainly will not have justice.* The Crown offers that, if you plead guilty, they will charge you with treason-felony; but if you refuse, you will be charged with high treason and many among you will be executed."[108]

That the Métis did not receive a just trial is also confirmed in a letter written to Macdonald by Henry Clarke, defence lawyer for the comrades of Riel.[109] Clarke was a political hack of Macdonald and was now seeking reward for his past services, amongst which was his role in the conviction of Riel. The letter refers to "the French half-breeds who had been forced to plead guilty". He continues to further implicate himself and other unnamed persons who were the cause of the resistance and subsequent execution of Riel.

> I think you can without much difficulty guess who is the author of the depositions of Pères André, Fourmond, Coucheau, Charles Nolin and others — all of which have been or ought to have been of great use to the government, placing as they do all the responsibility of the Rebellion on Riel and others and all condemning him without stint.
>
> . . . .
>
> I know every man of any importance in any way mixed up with the Rebellion, every man who took an open or secret part in goading the ignorant half-breeds into rebellion, the personal object of every man of any importance in getting up the Rebellion.[110]

These examples, a few of many, are conclusive evidence to portray the political and speculative motivations which embroil themselves in the reasons for the armed resistance and in the politically-motivated trial and subsequent execution of Riel.

The words of Dr. Howard Adams best describes this whole miscarriage of justice:

> The trial was held within the mechanics and rules of the judicial system, at least as far as was obvious to the public. However, beyond that, it seems to have unfolded according to intrigues and conspiracies, collaborations and collusions among the power politicians and the capitalists with their vested interests.[111]

2. **The Judge**

The orchestrator of the trial was Judge Richardson, and as pointed out on page 10 supra, he was a government employee as well as being affiliated with the Orange Lodge. In his capacity as legal adviser to the government, Richardson gave several opinions with

---

108 *Ibid.* (Emphasis added)
109 Public Archives of Canada, Macdonald Papers, Vol. 110, No. 44779.
110 *Ibid.*
111 Adams, *Prison of Grass,* 1975, at 124-125.

regard to matters in the Territories. One such memo was forwarded to Colonel Dennis, Deputy Minister of the Interior, in 1880.[112] In this memo Richardson tends to show a bias towards "the evil influences of leading spirits of the Manitoba troubles of 1870, who, during the past season, have been traversing the country, doing at least "no good".[113] It is notorious that Riel was, according to people like Richardson, the prime moving spirit of the "Manitoba troubles". There is also reference to the fact that Richardson's house was accidently destroyed during the excitement at Fort Battleford.[114] It is therefore certainly questionable, if in fact Riel was tried by an impartial judge.

3. **The Jury**

The jury that decided the fate of Riel was composed of six persons, the legality of which is described on page 12 supra. The questionable aspect in this case is the fact that in a population as found in the Territories, the six jurors selected were all English-speaking Protestants. According to Charlebois, Richardson broke the traditional method of jury selection by drawing up a list of 36 people of his own choice, only five of which were French-Canadians or Catholic.[115]

Not much is known or written about the members of the jury. In a short article in the Saskatoon Star Phoenix, the feelings of one of the jurors, Francis Cosgrave, are outlined by his granddaughter:

> Mrs. Sivell said her father had considerable sympathy for the Métis leader and regarded the death sentence as a great injustice.[116]

A more startling statement was made by juror Edwin Brooks in a 1925 interview:

> . . . We (the jury) tried Louis Riel for treason but he was hanged for the murder of Thomas Scott.[117]

Although the jury recommended mercy, there was apprehension in certain quarters as to the impartiality of an all white, English-Protestant panel. In a letter to Taché on August 3, 1885, Carey stated that all the halfbreeds would plead guilty to the lesser charge of treason-felony, which is good because, "Regina juries being very

---

[112]Sessional Papers (No. 116), 48 Victoria 1885, at 80.
[113]*Ibid.*, at 81.
[114]*Supra,* note 9, at 220.
[115]*Ibid.*, 220-221.
[116]Accent, Thursday, March 27, 1975, at 4.
[117]*Supra,* note 9, at 227.

hostile".[118] This statement is probably justified on the basis that "race prejudice and passions were running high".[119]

This situation may best be described by the following quote from the book, *Hanged in Error,* by Leslie Hale:

> The case of Edith Thompson shows, as do many others, that the case of 'the woman taken in adultery' was once, before British juries, as difficult to defend as that of a Negro Communist before twelve 'good men and true' of Alabama.[120]

This possibly may be too harsh a statement; however, the fact is that Riel was not given the right to be tried by his peers. The jury, however, as individuals, appear to place the blame of the resistance movement into the government's lap, where it rightly belonged. As stated by one of the jurors in a letter:

> . . . had the Government done their duty and redressed the grievances of the half-breeds of Saskatchewan . . . there would never have been a second Riel rebellion, and consequently no prisoner to try and condemn.[121]

4. **The Trial Proper**

As outlined on page 4, supra, Riel was formally charged on July 6, 1885, and arraigned on July 20, 1885. This would have left the defense with only 14 days to prepare for the arraignment. As well, Riel's voluntary surrender occurred on May 15, 1885; he was delivered to the Regina Mounted Police station on May 23, 1885.[122] Riel was thus afforded less than two months to face his arraignment. Although Riel was penniless, a Defence Committee, located in the province of Quebec, was established and defence counsel retained.

It is, of course, apparent that the raising of funds and the hiring of counsel would take time, as well as their preparation to meet the charge. It was because of this lack of proper opportunity to prepare that the Defence requested a one-month adjournment.[123]

It is also interesting to note that the Defence, prior to asking for the adjournment, had been frustrated in their attempts to interview potential witnesses because they had been instructed, either by the

---

[118]*Supra*, note 10, at 417, footnote 9.
[119]*Supra*, note 86, at 232.
[120]Leslie Hale, *Hanged in Error*, 1961, at 10.
[121]*Supra*, note 1.
[122]See page 4.
[123]*Supra*, note 3, at 49.

Prosecution or by someone for the Government, not to speak to the defence lawyers.[124]

The Defence in asking for the adjournment also made a formal request that the Court subpoena potential witnesses for the defence and that their costs be defrayed by the court.[125] This, of course, was because Riel had no money to meet the expenses. The Court, however, stated that they could not do so, as they had no funds.

The court was also informed that three necessary and important defence witnesses had sought asylum in the U.S.A. and that they were willing to testify on the basis that they were granted immunity.[126] However, this would take some time to arrange. These witnesses were required to establish Riel's American citizenship and his true purpose in returning to Saskatchewan, i.e., the legal and constitutional fight for Métis rights and upon the invitation of the Métis.

To also prove this point the defence requested the court to order all documents, petitions, etc., presented to the government by the Métis for the redress of their grievances.[127] These documents were in the hands of the Deputy Minister of the Interior and of Lawrence Vankoughnet, Deputy Superintendent of Indian Affairs. It is noteworthy that Vankoughnet in April, 1885, during the resistance, forwarded the numerous letters and petitions to the Department of the Interior.

> Ottawa, 21st April, 1885.
>
> My Dear Mr. Burgess, I forward to you the following files of this Department: 2094, 3559, 4041, 4145, 4953, 10766, 12014. These files contain correspondence referring more or less to half-breed matters in the Northwest Territories. They have been culled from an immense number of other files on Indian matters, and I think they should properly have been retained in the Department of the Interior.
>
> Very truly yours,
> L. Vankoughnet[128]

These letters and petitions cover the period from 1873 to 1885, and would have been an excellent source to outline the Métis grievances. Nevertheless, this material was never produced and if it had been, would have been argued as inadmissible by the Prosecution.[129]

---

[124] *Ibid.*
[125] *Ibid.*, at 46.
[126] *Ibid.*, at 47.
[127] *Ibid.*
[128] *Supra*, note 112, at 1.
[129] *Supra*, note 3, at 54.

In the final analysis, the Defence was only granted a one-week adjournment which in a trial of this nature and physical setting, surely amounts to a denial of natural justice.

There appears to have been a relaxed attitude by the judge in entertaining hearsay evidence, which at one point was objected to by the Defence.[130] That the Judge was biased, however, is much more flagrant.[131] This especially is portrayed in his charge to the jury, which was highly prejudicial.[132]

> My intention now is to read the evidence which has been taken. I feel it my duty to do so, from the way it has been given, and after I have read it, to draw your attention to it *and to make a few observations that occur to me, which may be useful to yourselves in arriving at a conclusion*.[133]

One of the conclusions he observed and in reality reached for the jury was the "fact" that a rebellion had occurred.

> The questions really for you to determine are first: Are you satisfied that there was a rebellion? If you are satisfied that there was a rebellion, *as I think you must be*, . . .[134]

Not only did he conclude this fact for the jury, he suggested to them that Riel's insanity, if in fact he was insane, started in December and not in March as was argued by the Defence.

> I only *suggest* that to you, not that you are to take it as law; I merely *suggest* it to you as turning upon the evidence.[135]

Then, to ensure that the jury could not possibly acquit Riel, Richardson made it clear that the blame and ill-feelings generated by the Métis Resistance and Indian retaliation would be shifted to them.

> On you rests the responsibility of pronouncing upon the guilt or innocence of the prisoner at the bar. Not only must you think of the man in the dock, but you must think of society at large; you are not called upon to think of the Government at Ottawa simply as a Government; you have to think of the homes and of the people who live in this country; you have to ask yourselves. Can such things be permitted?[136]

But, are the Judge and the Prosecutors the only blameworthy participants? There appears to be reasonable grounds now to doubt the effectiveness of the Defence. This is especially so in light of the fact that their sole defence was insanity, whereas Riel did everything in his

---

[130] *Ibid.*, at 148.
[131] See pages 10 and 81.
[132] *Supra*, note 3, at 343.
[133] *Ibid.*, at 344. (Emphasis added)
[134] *Ibid.*, at 346. (Emphasis added)
[135] *Ibid.*, at 348. (Emphasis added)
[136] *Ibid.*, at 349.

power to convince the judge and the jury of his sanity. Riel wanted to rely on the history and reasons for the Métis stand. This, however, was denied him. In fact, when Riel tried to contest the validity of Nolin's testimony, his lawyers made it clear that they would withdraw if Riel was allowed to question the witnesses.[137] Riel was, from that point forward, at the mercy and control of all the players in the court.

Riel, in his address to the Court after his verdict of guilty, reviewed the history of his and the Métis nation's struggle.[138] Riel's address certainly displayed his understanding of International Law and the basis upon which he had acted from 1869 to 1885. He also, in a limited fashion, outlined the legitimate grievances of the Métis and of the government inaction. The matters he spoke of certainly would have reflected adversely upon the government's administration in the Northwest. This would have been relayed to all major centers of the world. This is possibly one reason why the Defence chose to rely solely on the insanity defence. From our research it appears that Riel's defence fund came from French-Canadian Liberals who aspired to national prominence. It is, therefore, quite conceivable that the defence of Riel as a political showpiece was desirable, but had to be done without dragging out the sordid details which would reflect upon the whole of white society against the colonized native.

Whatever the reasons or motivations of the Defence not to acquiesce to Riel's wishes and line of defence, there is no reason why the jury was not asked why they felt that Riel should be shown mercy by the Crown.

The Defence was also derelict in their duty in not basing their appeal to the Manitoba Court of Queen's Bench on other errors, in addition to the constitutional issue and the insanity question.[139] The Defence certainly could have argued bias, but more importantly, the issue of the judge's prejudicial charge to the jury. As was erroneously stated by Chief Justice Wallbridge:

> The prisoner was defended by able counsel, and all evidence called which he desired. No complaint is now made as to unfairness, haste, or want of opportunity of having all the evidence heard which he desired to have heard.[140]

It is quite apparent from the preceding remarks that Riel was

---

[137]*Ibid.*, at 209.
[138]*Ibid.*, at 350.
[139]*Supra*, note 13, at 26.
[140]*Ibid.*, at 25.

never afforded the opportunity to present the evidence which he believed should be relied upon. In addition, there is certainly every reason to indicate the "haste" of the court to try Riel.

C. THE RECOMMENDATION OF MERCY

Although the jury was forced to find Riel guilty of high treason, they nevertheless realized that the death penalty was not justified because of the surrounding circumstances of which, as residents of the Northwest Territories, they would have been aware.[141]

Macdonald, however, for reasons explained earlier, was determined not to act on this recommendation and in fact completely disregarded it.

---

[141]See page 82, supra.

VII.

From Execution to Today

In the almost 100 years that have passed since the execution, Riel has gained the status of a martyr, not only among his people but among Canadians generally. His role in agitating for western rights is now generally recognized by Western Provinces. Both Saskatchewan and Manitoba have remembered him by erecting statues in his honour. His life and the events surrounding him have been studied more, written about more, reproduced more often in drama, than that of any other historical figure in Western Canada and possibly in all of Canada.[142] This is surely a recognition of the justice of his cause and the glaring miscarriage of justice toward the native people by the Macdonald regime and the Eastern establishment.

Riel has continued to be an inspiration to his people over the years. This is true today more than ever before, as a new awareness and understanding of their history and culture is instilled in our people. If we are to once again take our rightful place in Western Canadian society as founders of western economy and culture, and if we are to participate fully in the social, political and economic life of the area, it is important to nurture this awareness so that the people's sense of pride and their belief in themselves can be strengthened. We will, as a people, only be able to throw off the bonds of our poverty if we once again feel responsible for our own destiny and if we are given the opportunity to exercise our rights. An important way in which the Canadian government can recognize the wrongs of the past and help our people build their strength for the future is to remove the blot of "criminal" from the otherwise unblemished record of this gentle and just man who has become the personification of leadership and inspiration among our people.

---

[142]Dhand, Hunt and Goshawk, *Louis Riel, An Annotated Bibliography*, 1972. Although this booklet does not represent all the material, it includes a wide variety up to 1972.

VIII.

Pardon: A Royal Prerogative

Error is possible in all judgments. In every other case of judicial error, compensation can be made to the injured person. Death admits of no compensation.

Jeremy Bentham.[143]

A. HISTORICAL ASPECT

The Crown enjoys the exclusive right of granting pardons, a privilege which cannot be claimed by any other person either by grant or prescription. Throughout the Middle Ages the English kings had to contend, like their continental counterparts, with the rival powers of the feudal lords. This contest ended in the 16th century with the revival of supreme royal power, including the sole power of the Crown to pardon or remit any treason or felony.

Later, as Parliament grew stronger, this pardon authority was shared; the power of the Crown did not prevent pardons from being granted by Acts of Parliament. Today in England, the Crown's power is exercised for the royal sovereign by the Home Secretary.[144] In countries like Canada, this power is usually delegated to colonial governors and to Governors-General, although in doing so, the sovereign does not entirely divest herself of the prerogative.[145]

The Crown's authority to grant pardons was one aspect of a more general power to determine what punishment should be imposed for a particular category of offences and to remit or commute the prescribed penalty in individual cases.[146] All civilized countries make use of some form of the pardon power to give flexibility to the administration of justice in criminal cases.[147]

---

[143]Calvert, *Capital Punishment in the Twentieth Century*, 1971.
[144]Rubin, *Law of Criminal Correction*, 1973, at 673.
[145]8 Halsbury (4th, at 949).
[146]Hurnard, *The King's Pardon for Homicide, before A.D. 1307*, 1969, at 1.
[147]Newman, *Source Book on Probation. Parole and Pardons*, 1968, at 56.

B. PURPOSE AND EFFECT

There are basically two kinds of pardons: (1) Free pardons which are granted on the grounds of innocence established and admitted by the Crown; and (2) ordinary pardons which are granted on special consideration. Both kinds of pardon proceed from the same source as an act of grace, but the first is an act of grace to which the recipient is morally entitled, while the second is a pure act of grace.

A free pardon says, in effect, that the person to whom it is granted did not commit the offence of which he was convicted; that is, there has been a total miscarriage of justice.

In the case of ordinary pardons, the question of the guilt of the applicant for relief is not in issue. The possibility of a doubt as to guilt may, however, as a result of the inquiry, be found to exist. The special considerations upon which the service recommends an ordinary pardon are of various types depending on the facts.

The greatest number of applications received by the service for ordinary pardons is from persons who are prohibited from entering, remaining in or re-entering other countries because of past convictions. The conviction may have been long-standing and the applicant may have led, since the conviction, a consistently law-abiding and respectable life.[148]

The Crown's pardon, if general in its purport and sufficient in other respects, obliterates every stain which the law attached to the offender. Generally speaking, it puts him in the same situation as that in which he stood before he committed the pardoned offence and frees him from the penalties and forfeitures to which the law subjected his person and property. Though a pardon cannot wash away those doubts with which the evidence of one who has committed a serious offence will be received, yet, in point of law, a legal pardon implies a removal of the stigma, restores a man to credit and enables him to bring an action against anyone who scandalizes him in respect of the crime pardoned.[149]

C. PROVISIONS FOR PARDONS AND PROCEDURE

From the same principle that gave to a subject the right of discharging an appeal he had brought before a court of justice, the

---

[148]McGrath, *Crime and its Treatment in Canada,* 1965 at 102.
[149]Chitty, *Prerogatives of the Crown,* 1968, at 102.

lawyers have derived the prerogative of mercy enjoyed by the Crown. As representative of the state, the Sovereign may frustrate by his pardon an indictment prosecuted in his name. In every crime that affects the public he is the injured person in the eye of the law, and may therefore, it is said, pardon an offence which is held to have been committed against himself.[150]

> S.683 of the Criminal Code of Canada states:[151]
>
> s. 683 (1) Her Majesty may extend the royal mercy to a person who is sentenced to imprisonment under the authority of an Act of the parliament of Canada, even if the person is imprisoned for failure to pay money to another person.
>
> (2) The Governor-in-Council may grant a free pardon or a conditional pardon to any person who has been convicted of an offence.
>
> (3) Where the Governor-in-Council grants a free pardon to a person, that person shall be deemed thereafter never to have committed the offence in respect of which the pardon is granted.
>
> (4) No free pardon or conditional pardon prevents or mitigates the punishment to which the person might otherwise be lawfully sentenced on a subsequent conviction for an offence other than that for which the pardon was granted.
>
> s.686 Nothing in this Act in any manner limits or affects Her Majesty's royal prerogative of mercy.

The *Criminal Code* authorizes the Governor-General-in-Council to grant relief from punishment to offenders. This can be done by remitting part of the sentence of imprisonment, by granting a free pardon or conditional pardon, or by remitting, in whole or in part, a pecuniary penalty, fine or forfeiture imposed under an Act of Parliament. However, as has been noted, nothing in the *Criminal Code* in any manner limits or affects Her Majesty's royal prerogative of mercy. The traditional practice in Canada has been for the Governor-General, acting on the advice of one member of the Cabinet, to exercise the royal prerogative of mercy where the punishment in respect of which it is sought is a punishment other than death.[152]

A pardon other than a pardon under statute must be specially pleaded at the first opportunity the defendant has of doing so. If he has obtained a pardon before arraignment and, instead of pleading it, pleads only the general issue, he is deemed to have waived the benefit of pardon. If a pardon is granted after the plea is pleaded, advantage

---

[150]Allen, *The Royal Prerogative in England*, 1849, at 108.
[151]R.S.C. 1970, c. C-34, s.s. 683 and 686.
[152]*Supra*, note 148, at 102-103.

of it may be taken at any time after verdict in arrest of judgment, and after judgment in arrest of execution.[153]

A proclamation promising pardon does not have the legal effect of a pardon but following such a proclamation the court will defer execution of sentence and so allow time for the prisoner to apply for a pardon.[154]

D. ERRORS OF JUSTICE — POSTHUMOUS PARDON

History is full of tragic stories in which innocent people have been condemned. The Adolf Beck case will be remembered by many as an extraordinary instance of wrongful conviction. He was sentenced in 1896 to seven years penal servitude for a series of robberies from women, was released after five years, and in 1904 was re-arrested and again convicted for further offences of a similar character. On the first occasion he was identified by no less than ten women, and at the second trial by five women, each of whom swore to his identity as the man who swindled her; a handwriting expert called by the prosecution at each trial testified on oath that letters written by the real culprit were in Beck's handwriting; two prison officials wrongly identified Beck as a previously convicted man — Smith — who was afterwards proved to be the real perpetrator of the crimes for which Beck was found guilty. Rarely has evidence been so overwhelming as it was in this case, yet Beck was subsequently discovered to be absolutely innocent. "There is no shadow of foundation," stated the official report, "for any of the charges made against Mr. Beck." The Home Office awarded him 5,000 pounds compensation. Yet it took Adolf Beck nine years to establish his innocence; had he been convicted of a capital offence and executed in consequence instead of imprisoned, the error would probably never have come to light. There is obviously far less chance of discovering a miscarriage of justice when a person is executed, since he is no longer able to prosecute his claim. Yet many people have been sent to the scaffold on evidence far less overwhelming than that upon which Beck was wrongfully convicted.

The importance of the Beck case is twofold. (1) The fact that evidence so overwhelming proved mistaken, should bring an element of doubt into nearly every trial and make the inflection of an

---

[153] 11 Halsbury (4th), at 240.
[154] *R.* v. *Rudd* (1775) 1 Leach 115.

irrevocable penalty unthinkable. (2) The fact that few errors of justice come to light in connection with capital offences should not lead us to suppose that such mistakes do not occur.[155]

Also in Lincolnshire in 1869, Priscilla Biggadyke was convicted of poisoning her husband, dragged to the scaffold and executed, protesting her innocence. Subsequently, a man on his death bed confessed that he had entered the kitchen and, unknown to Mrs. Biggadyke, put poison in the pudding she was making.[156]

Another striking example of a gross miscarriage of justice involved two men — Mr. Evans and Mr. Christie — and a large group of women, all of whom had been strangled.

In 1953, police found the remains of six female bodies in the garden and under the floorboards of a seedy tenement house at Number 10, Rillington Place in London. A former tenant of the house named John Reginald Halliday Christie confessed to having strangled the victims and buried their corpses. The press dubbed him, "The Monster of Rillington Place". He was tried, found guilty and sentenced to hang. There was an added aspect of the crime which set it apart from more commonplace murders. Christie had also confessed to having killed another former resident of the house, one Mrs. Evans. Unfortunately, her husband Timothy John Evans, had already been executed for that murder.

The case could not have been more bizarre. Evans was a virtually illiterate truck driver of very low intelligence who, one day in 1949, contacted police and confessed to the murder of his wife. Although he said he had stuffed the body into a drain, it was found in a wash house behind the house along with the body of Evans' only child. Both had died by strangling and a man's necktie was still in place around the child's neck. Evans later changed his story and alleged that Christie, who lived in the same house, had killed Mrs. Evans while performing an abortion on her. Christie denied any guilt in the matter and became the main witness for the prosecution. Evans' hanging followed an unsuccessful appeal.

Three years after Evans died, Christie strangled his own wife and chucked her body under the floorboards. His other victims were prostitutes whom he brought home, strangled, raped and buried.

---

[155]*Supra*, note 143, at 121-122.
[156]*Ivid.*, at 125.

Riel holding the scales of justice — Composite photo — C. Bunnie.

Police found a collection of their hair swatches, which the murderer kept in a tobacco tin. He was diagnosed as a fetishist and a necrophiliac. He alleged that during the war he had killed twenty-two other women whose bodies he later deposited on bomb sites. Details of the Grisly case horrified and fascinated the public. The murder of the

Evans' child was never fully explained but belief in Timothy Evans' wrongful conviction and exposure of the efforts of officials to conceal evidence turned the case into a powerful argument against the death penalty, which was abolished in Great Britain in 1965. Evans, who was not in a position to benefit from clemency, *was granted a posthumous pardon.*[157]

Mr. Chuter Ede, universally respected as a humanitarian, considered the case of Timothy John Evans. The case, as then presented, suggested no question of doubt, no reason for clemency. The decision he made was inevitable; but he earned still greater respect and sympathy when, in February, 1955, he courageously declared:

> "I was the Home Secretary who wrote on Evans' papers, 'The law must take its course.' I never said, in 1948, that a mistake was impossible. I think Evans' case shows, in spite of all that has been done since, that a mistake was possible. And that, in the form in which the verdict was actually given on a particular case, a mistake was made."[158]

---

[157]Horwitz, *Capital Punishment,* U.S.A., 1973, at 169-70. (Emphasis added)
[158]*Supra,* note 120, at 5.

IX.

A Pardon is in Order

We, therefore, request on behalf of all the Métis people and on behalf of others who look to Riel's example for inspiration, that the Canadian Government act immediately by exercising the Royal Prerogative of mercy and by conveying to the Métis organization a grant of pardon for Riel. As outlined under heading VIII, the government clearly has the authority to take such action. Although we know of no historical precedent in Canada for a posthumous pardon, the Imperial Parliament of Britain has provided the mechanism for it. The arguments in favour of such action are strong.

a) Riel acted out of the conviction that he was right in International Law to advocate the recognition of the rights of his people;

b) Riel did not act for reasons of personal gain or to enhance his own reputation;

c) Riel himself committed no illegal act either at the Red River or at Batoche;

d) Riel did not advocate war or armed resistance and only armed his people to enable them to protect themselves in the face of what they believed were hostile intentions toward them by the government;

e) The government could have avoided the violence and destruction by having indicated some preparedness to recognize the legitimate rights of the people and to negotiate a settlement;

f) When the violence did occur, it happened more by accident than as a result of any deliberate plan by Riel to have his people rise in armed revolt;

g) Riel consistently avoided using available military strategy to take advantage of government police and troops;

h) Riel did not receive a fair trial because of bias and prejudice toward him from many quarters;

i) The government ignored the jury's recommendation of mercy;

j) The government by such action today could renew the faith of the Métis people in the possibility of just treatment for themselves within Canadian society. This is especially important during the current movement for National Unity.

The granting of a posthumous pardon at this time will acknowledge the words of Riel, directed to the jury before they retired to consider their verdict, and officially accord him his rightful position in the development of the Canadian Nation.

> I am glad the Crown have proved that I am the leader of the half-breeds in the Northwest. I will perhaps be one day acknowledged as more than a leader of the half-breeds, and if I am, I will have an opportunity of being acknowledged *as a leader of good in this great country.*[159]

[159]*Supra*, note 3, at 321. (Emphasis added)

Bibliography

BOOKS

Auguste Trémaudan, edited by H. Adams, *History of the Mètis Nation.*

Burton Deane, *Mounted Police Life in Canada,* (Cassell and Co. Ltd., Toronto, 1916), reprinted by Coles Publishing Co., Toronto, 1973.

C. L. Newman, *Source Book on Probation, Parole and Pardons,* (C.C. Thomas Publishers, Springfield, Ill., 1968).

Calvert, *Capital Punishment in the Twentieth Century,* (Kennikat Press, New York, 1971).

Charlebois, *The Life of Louis Riel,* (New Canada Publications, Toronto, 1975).

D. Morton, *The Queen v. Louis Riel,* (University of Toronto Press, Toronto, 1974).

E. L. Horwitz, *Capital Punishment, U.S.A.,* (J.B. Lippincott Co., New York, 1973).

George F. G. Stanley, *Louis Riel,* (McGraw-Hill Ryerson Limited, Toronto, 1964).

George F. G. Stanley, *The Birth of Western Canada, A History of the Riel Rebellions,* (University of Toronto Press, Toronto, 1961).

Howard Adams, *Prison of Grass,* (New Press, Toronto, 1975).

Hurnard, *The King's Pardon for Homicide, before A.D. 1307,* (Clarendon Press, Oxford, 1969).

J. Chitty, *A Treatise on the Law of the Prerogative of the Crown,* (Gregg International Publishers Ltd., 1968).

John Allen, *The Royal Prerogative in England,* (Burt Frank, New York, 1849).

Joseph Howard, *Strange Empire, Louis Riel and the Mètis People,* (James Lewis and Samuel, Toronto, 1974).

Leslie Hale, *Hanged in Error,* (Penguin Books, 1961).

Manitoba Métis Federation, *Riverlots and Scrip, Elements of Métis Aboriginal Rights,* (Manitoba Métis Federation Inc., 1978).

McGrath, *Crime and Its Treatment in Canada,* (MacMillan of Canada, Toronto, 1965).

Rubin, *Law of Criminal Correction,* (West Publishing Co., St. Paul, Minn., 1973).

W. L. Morton, *Manitoba: The Birth of a Province,* (Manitoba Record Society Pub., Altona, 1965).

JOURNAL

Peter MacKinnon, Conspiracy and Sedition as Canadian Political Crimes (1977), 23 *McGill Law Journal* 622.

COMMISSION AND COMMITTEE REPORTS

British Parliamentary Papers, Anthropology Aborigines, *Report from the Select Committee on Aborigines (British Settlements) with Minutes of Evidence and Appendix and Index,* Volumes 1 and 2, Sessions 1836 and 1837.

British Parliamentary Papers, Anthropology Aborigines, *Correspondence and other Papers relating to Aboriginal Tribes in British Possessions, 1834.* Volume 3, session 1834.

British Parliament Papers, *Report of the Select Committee on Hudson's Bay Company,* Session 1857, Colonies Canada, Volume 3.

DEBATES

Canada, House of Commons Debates.

Canada, Sessional Papers.

OTHER REFERENCES

Association of Métis and Non-Status Indians of Saskatchewan Research Documents.

Charles Napier Bell, The Historical and Scientific Society of Manitoba, *The Old Forts of Winnipeg (1738-1927),* 1927.

Devrome, *The Métis, 1821-1885,* M. A. Thesis presented in 1976 to the Department of Anthropology, University of Alberta.

Dhand, Hunt and Goshawk, *Louis Riel, An Annotated Bibliography,* (Research Resources Centre, College of Education, Univ. of Saskatchewan, 1972).

Documents and Articles about Métis People, 1972, Saskatchewan Archives, Regina, Doc. J2P5.

H. C. Knox, *One Hundred Years Ago,* Public Archives of Manitoba.

Saskatoon Star-Phoenix, Accent, Thursday, March 27, 1975.